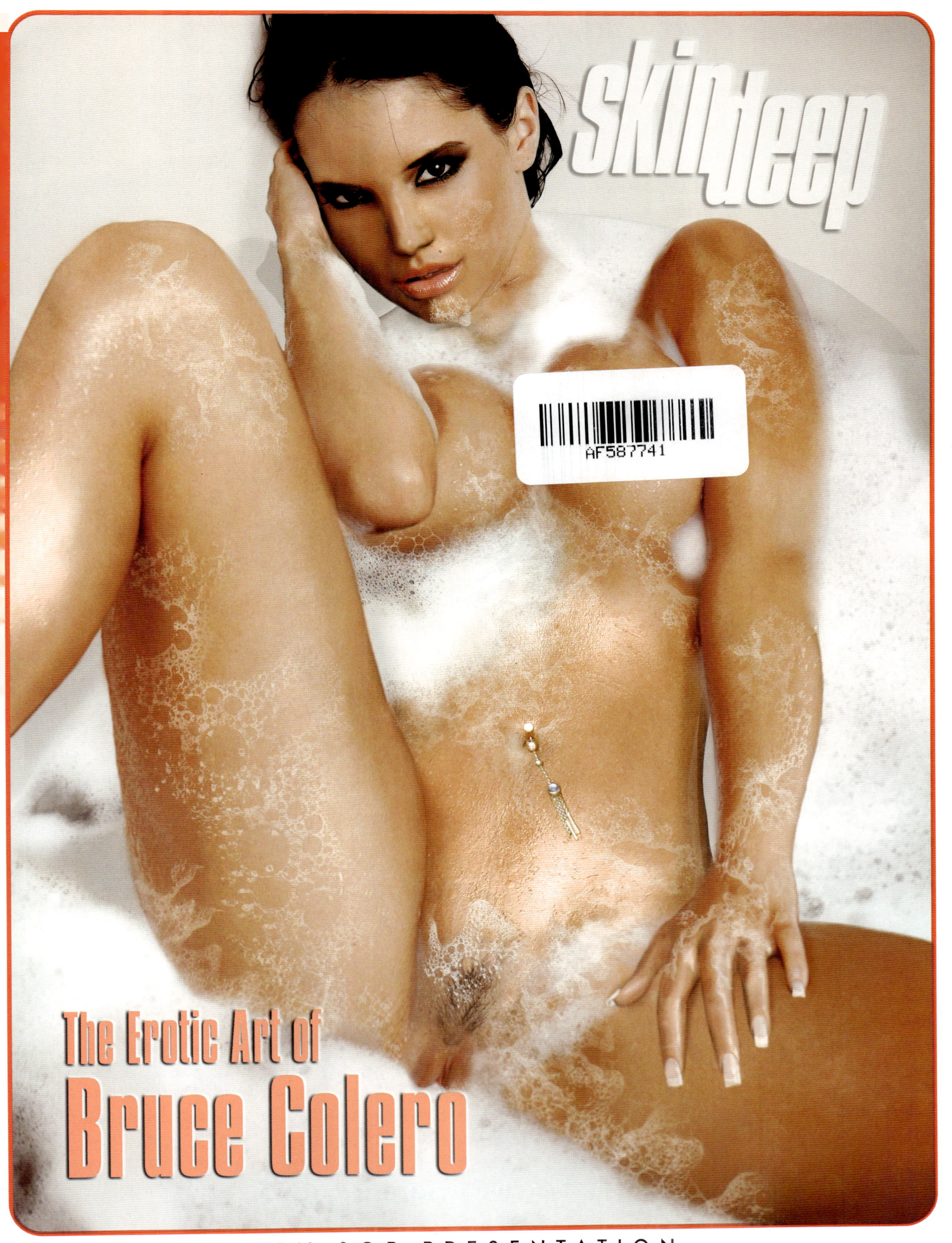

AN SQP PRESENTATION

Skin Deeper - Bruce Colero on Paint and Passion

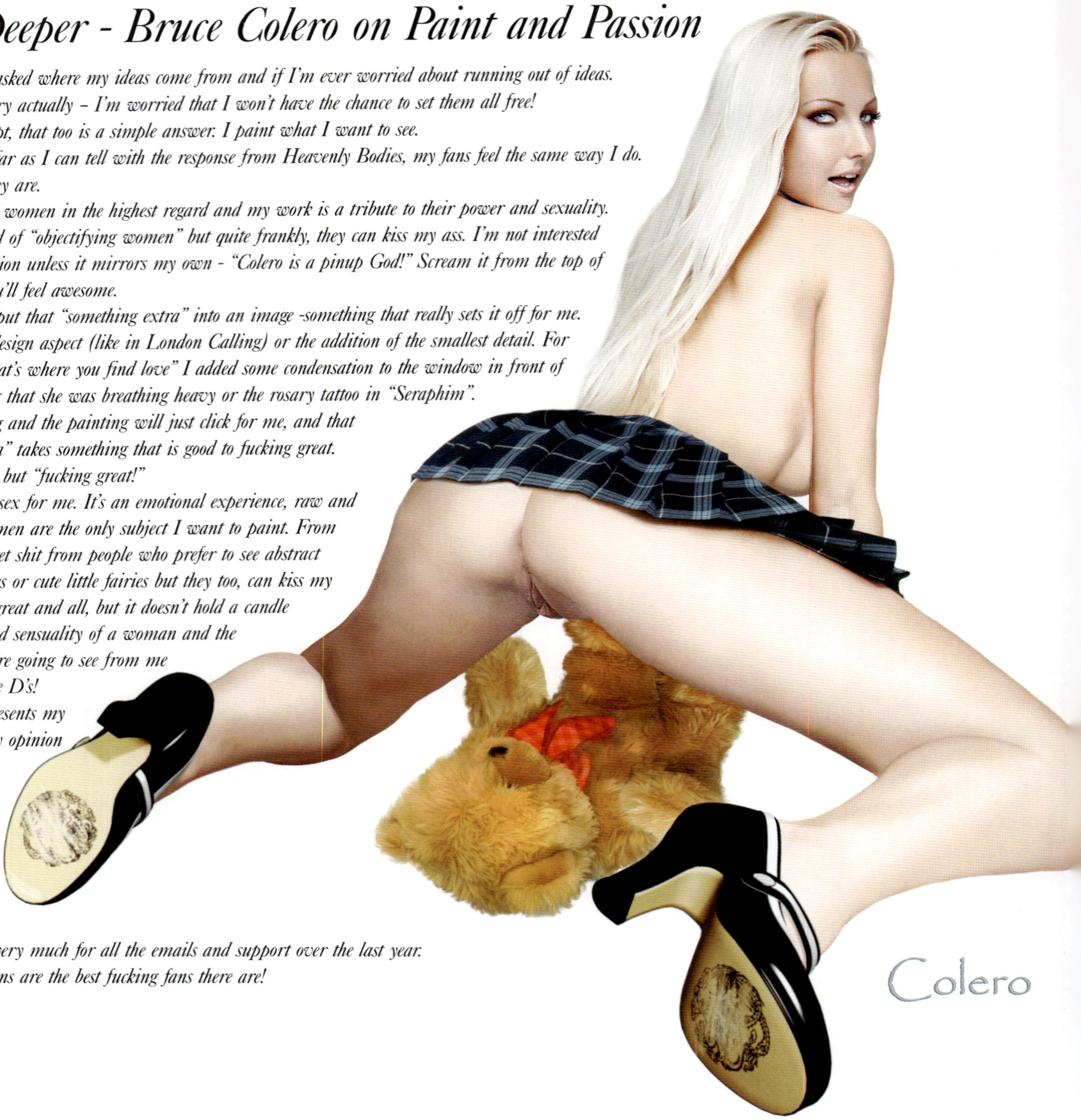

I constantly get asked where my ideas come from and if I'm ever worried about running out of ideas. Quite the contrary actually – I'm worried that I won't have the chance to set them all free! As for the concept, that too is a simple answer. I paint what I want to see. Fortunately, as far as I can tell with the response from Heavenly Bodies, my fans feel the same way I do. Perverts that they are.

I've always held women in the highest regard and my work is a tribute to their power and sexuality. I've been accused of "objectifying women" but quite frankly, they can kiss my ass. I'm not interested in anyone's opinion unless it mirrors my own - "Colero is a pinup God!" Scream it from the top of your lungs – you'll feel awesome.

I always try to put that "something extra" into an image -something that really sets it off for me. It could be the design aspect (like in London Calling) or the addition of the smallest detail. For example in "That's where you find love" I added some condensation to the window in front of her lips showing that she was breathing heavy or the rosary tattoo in "Seraphim". I'll do something and the painting will just click for me, and that "something extra" takes something that is good to fucking great. Not just "great" but "fucking great!"

Painting is like sex for me. It's an emotional experience, raw and primal and women are the only subject I want to paint. From time to time I get shit from people who prefer to see abstract art or landscapes or cute little fairies but they too, can kiss my ass. Scenery is great and all, but it doesn't hold a candle to the beauty and sensuality of a woman and the only fairies you're going to see from me will have double D's!

Skin Deep represents my latest and in my opinion my best work; certainly my most sexual. I hope you get off on the images as much as I did.

Lastly, thanks very much for all the emails and support over the last year. Bruce Colero fans are the best fucking fans there are!

Best,
Bruce Colero
2008

Colero

Skin Deep
The Erotic Art of Bruce Colero
Volume One

Book design by Grassy Knoll Studios.

Published by
SQP Inc.
PO Box 248 - Columbus, NJ 08022

Sal Quartuccio & Bob Keenan - Publishers

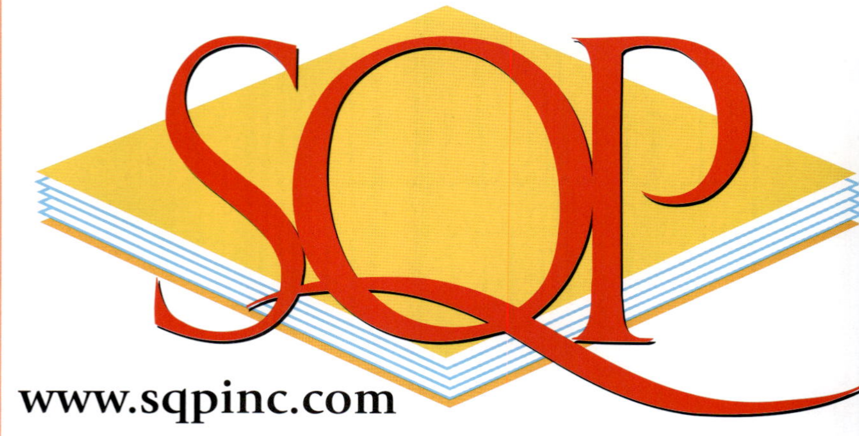

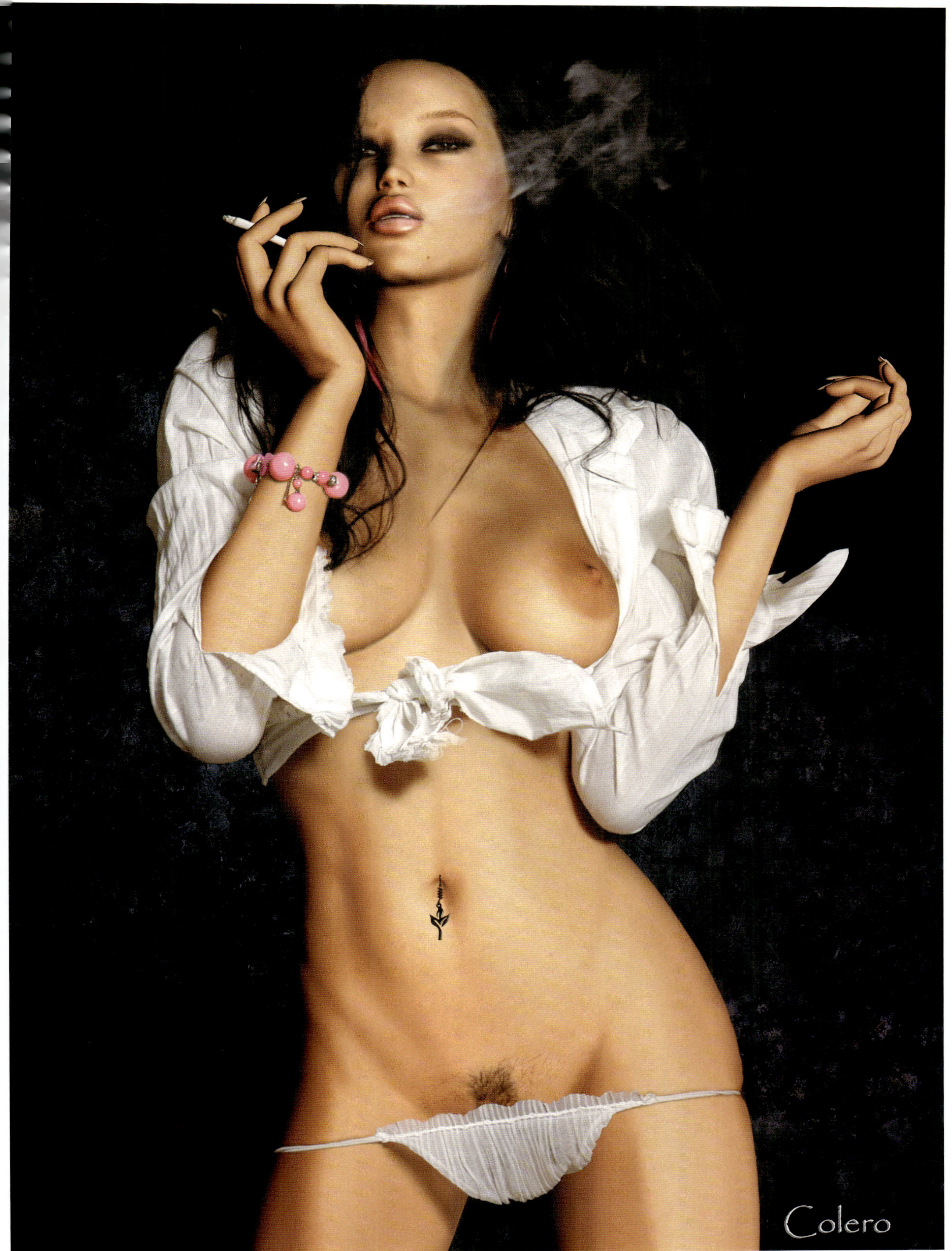

Bad Girl

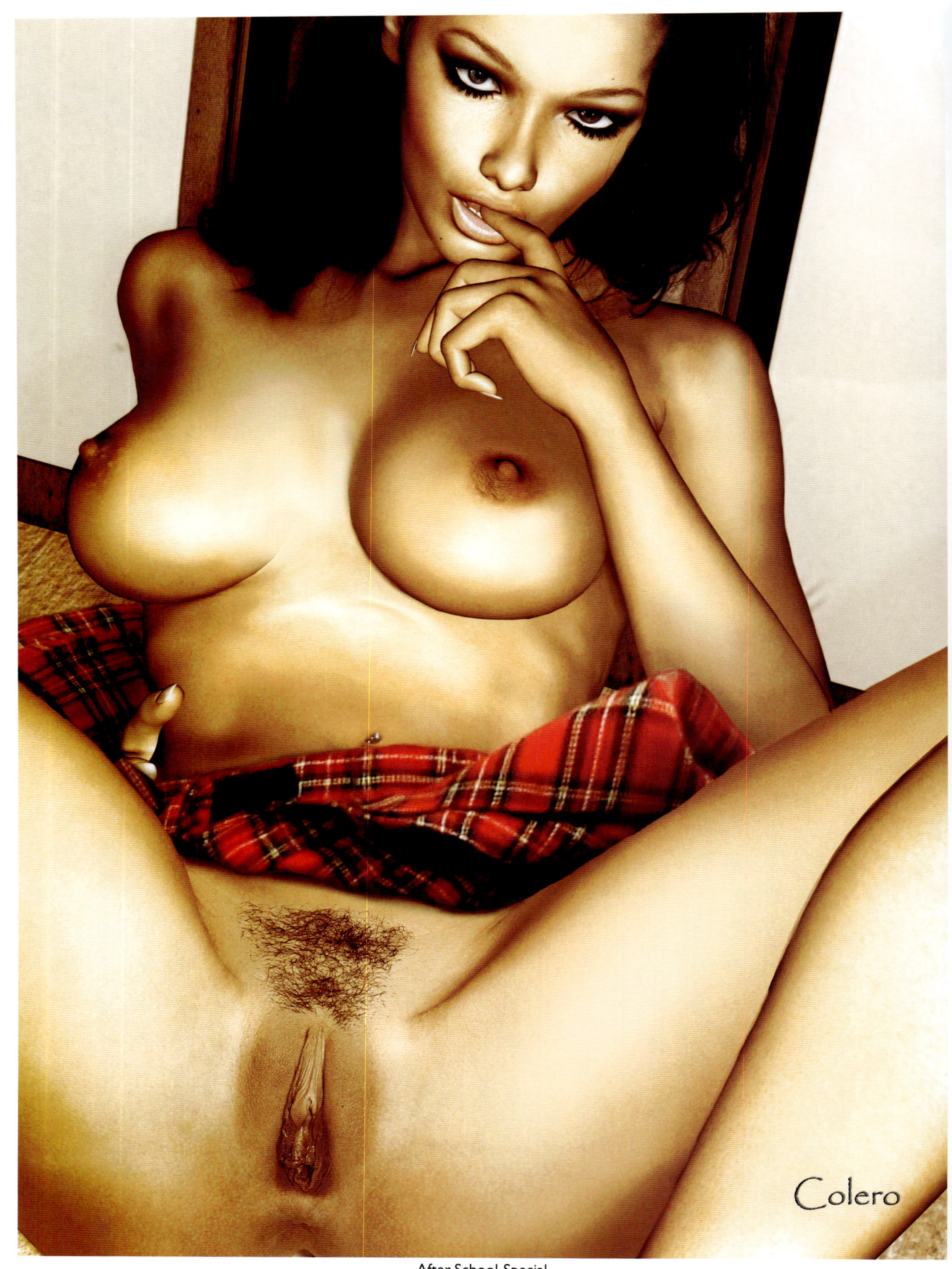

After School Special

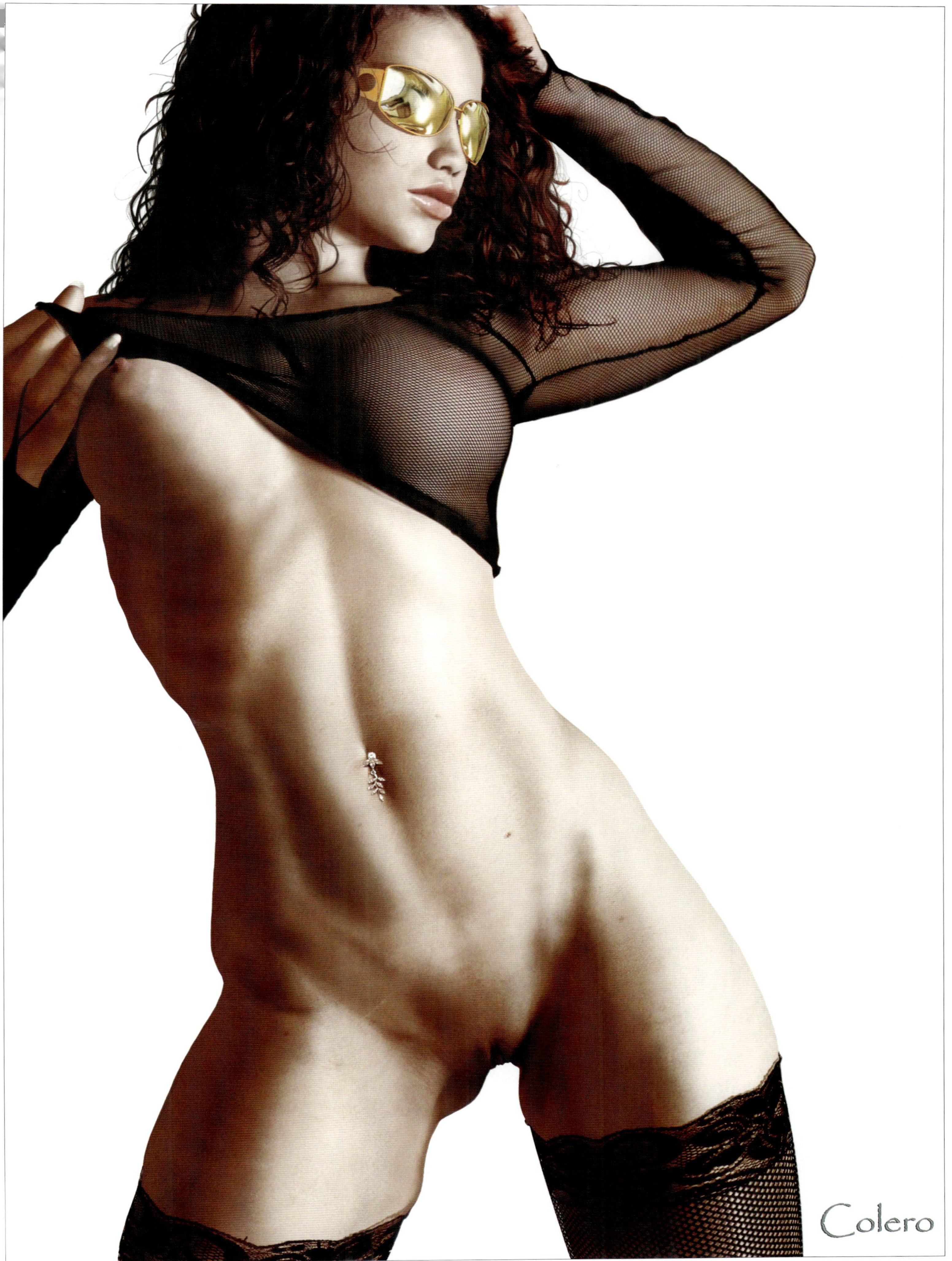

Superbad

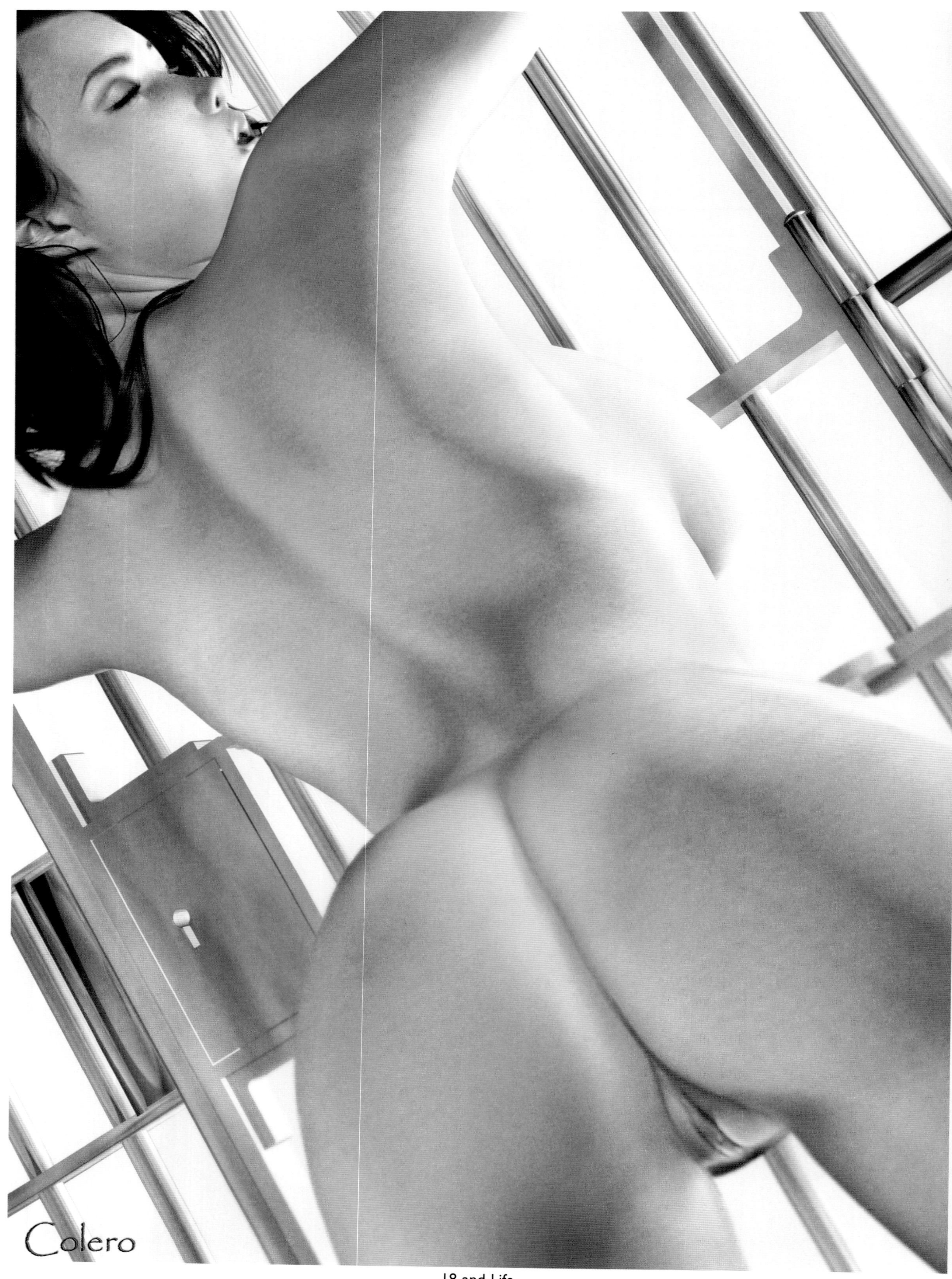
Colero

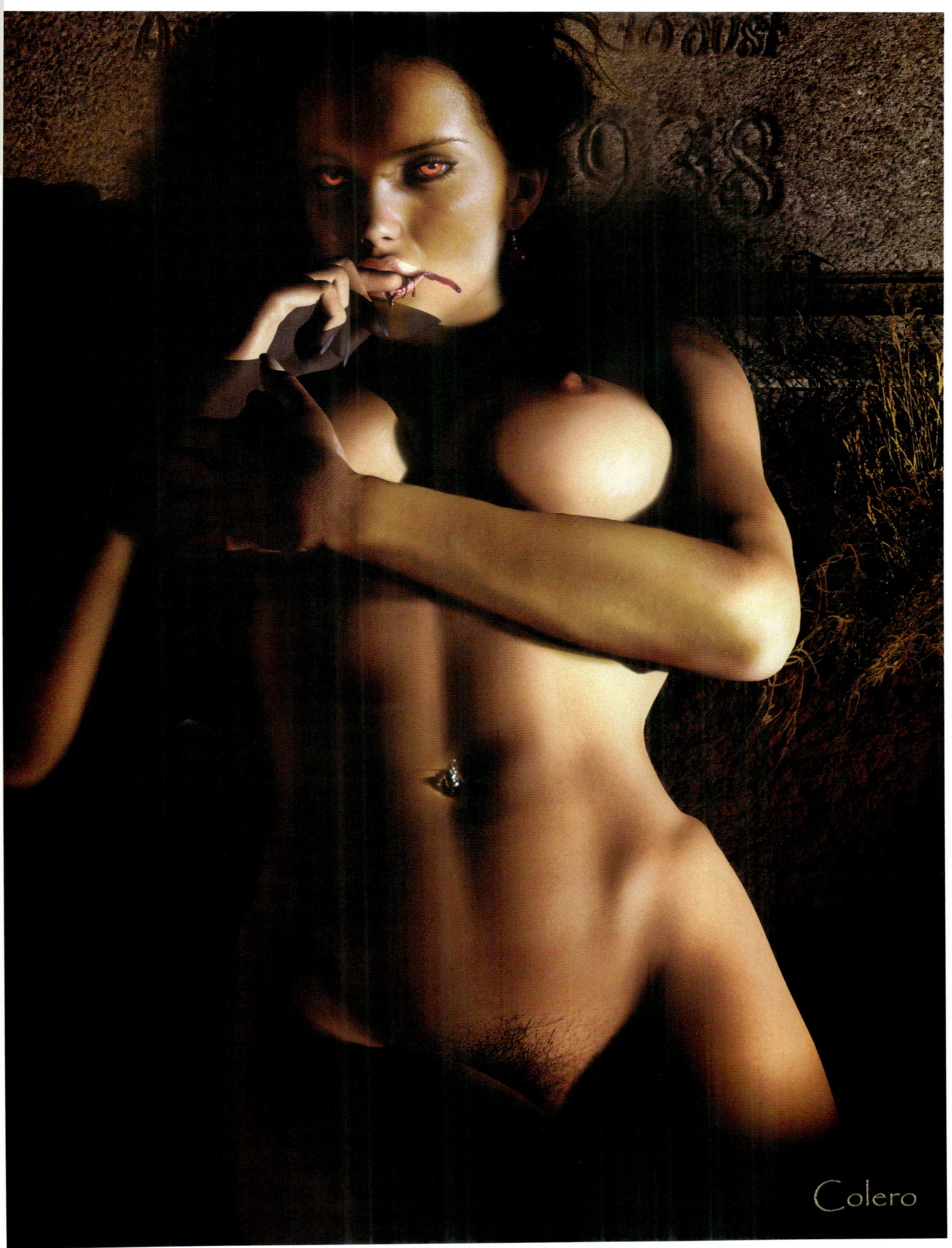

Les Morts Dansant

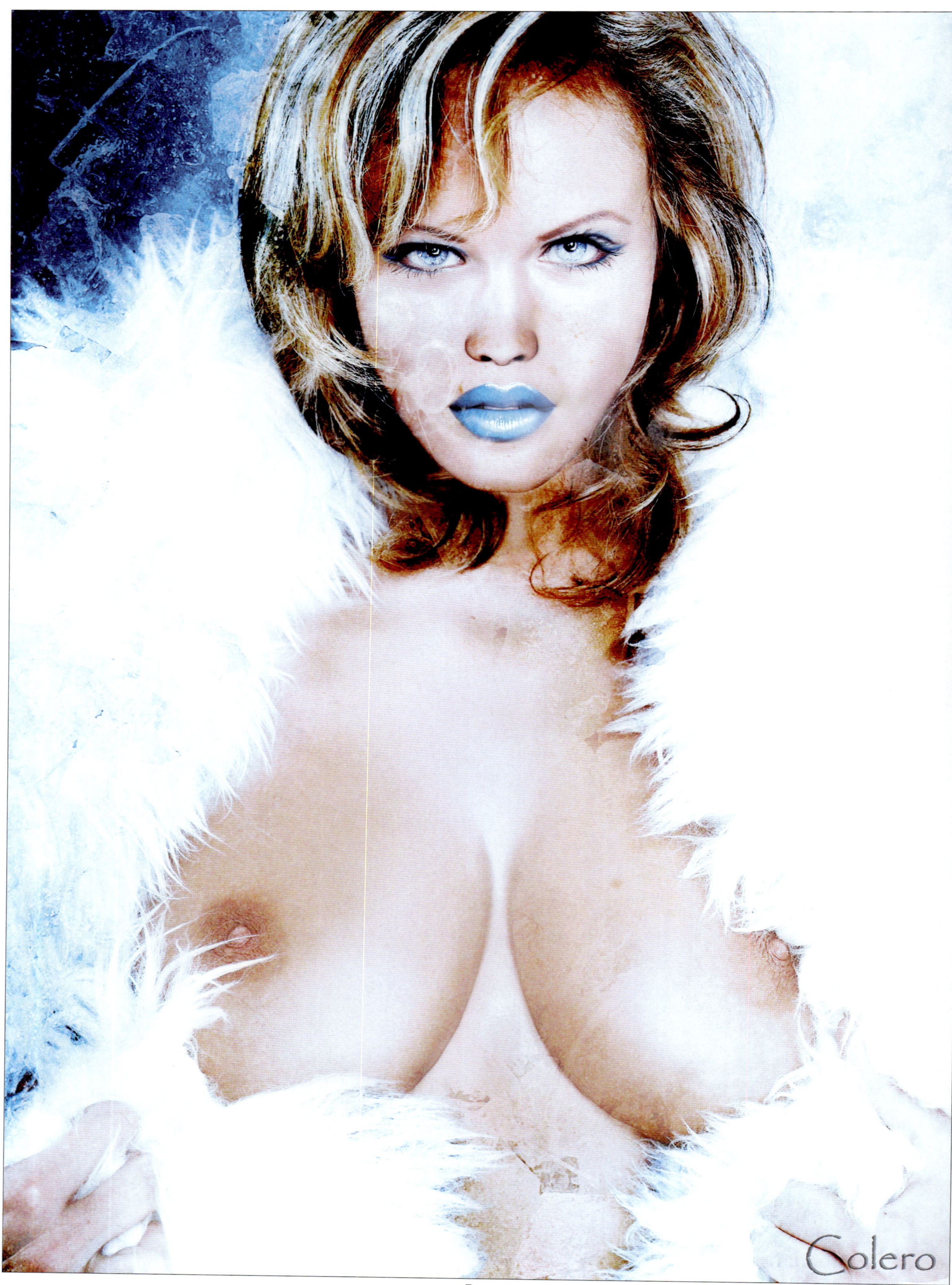

Fur

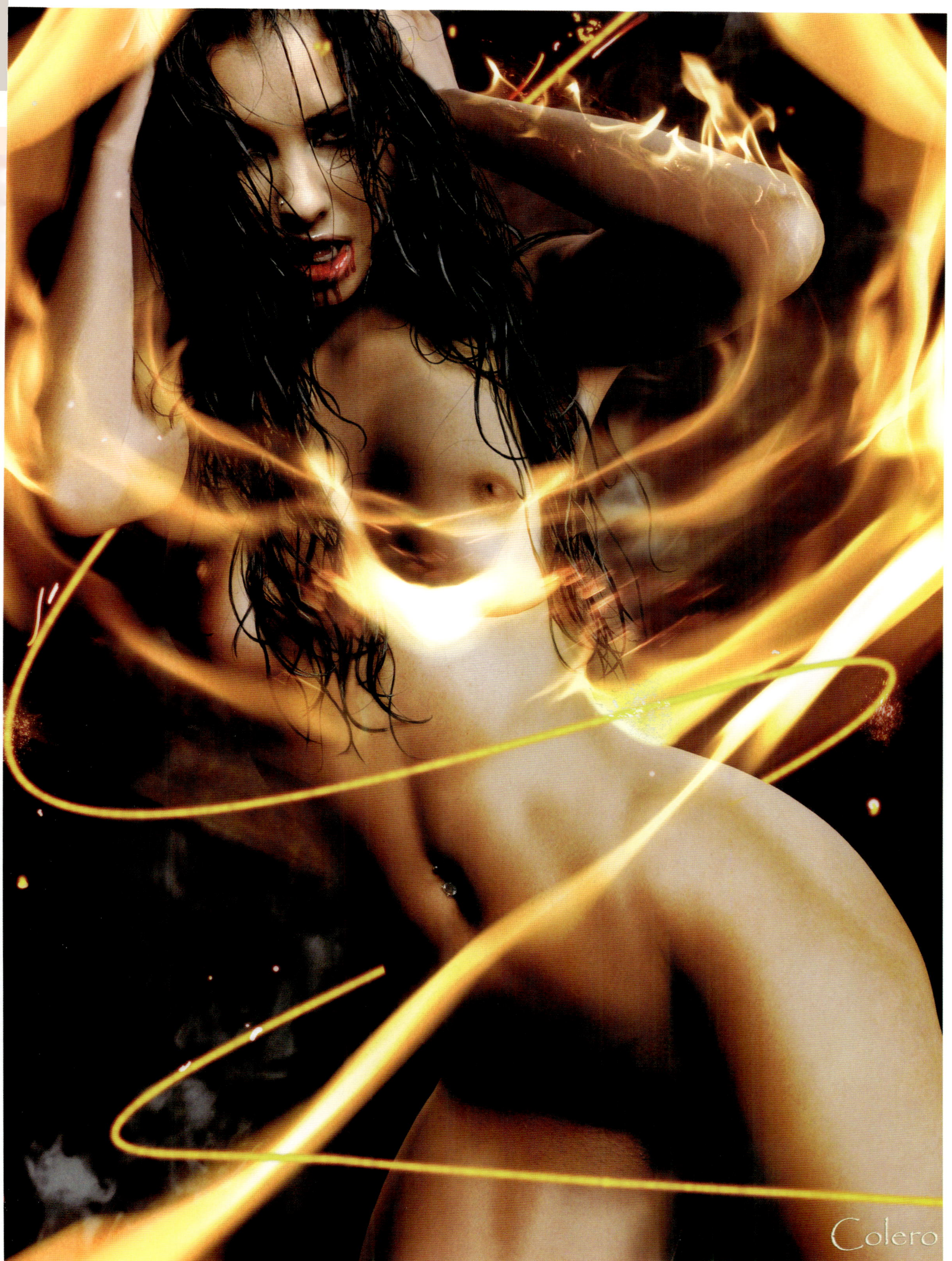

Daughter of Darkness

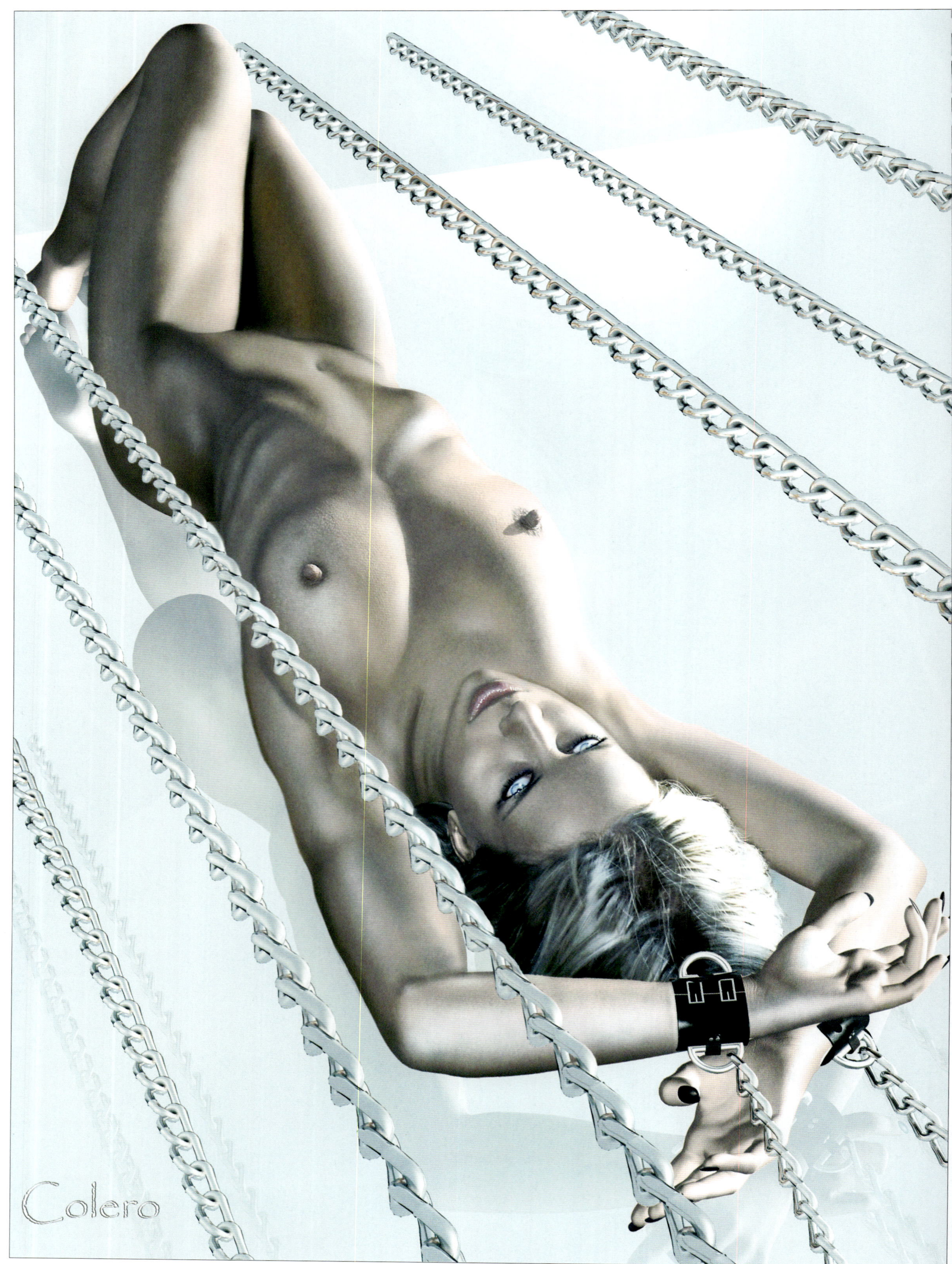

Do What Thou Will

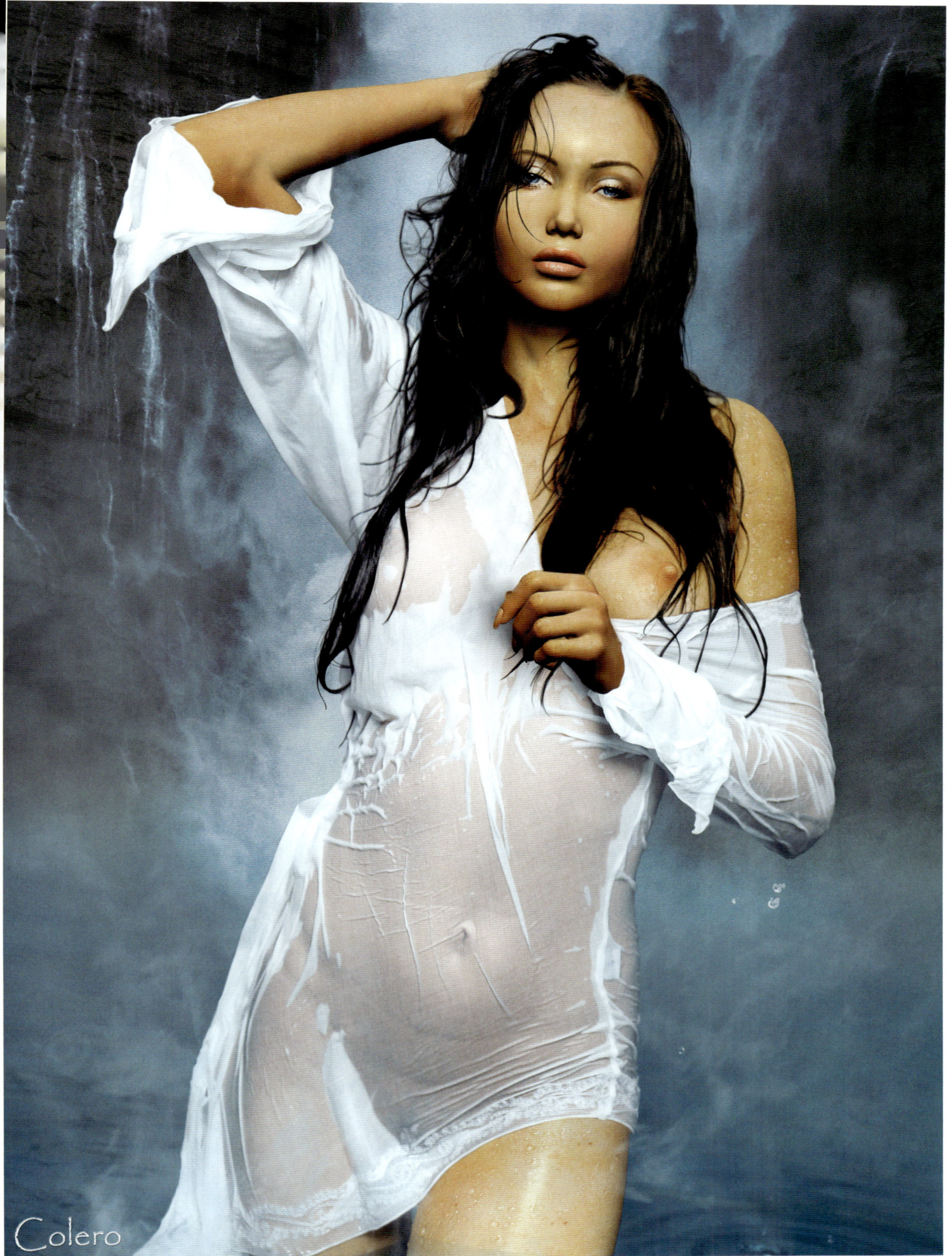

Teflis

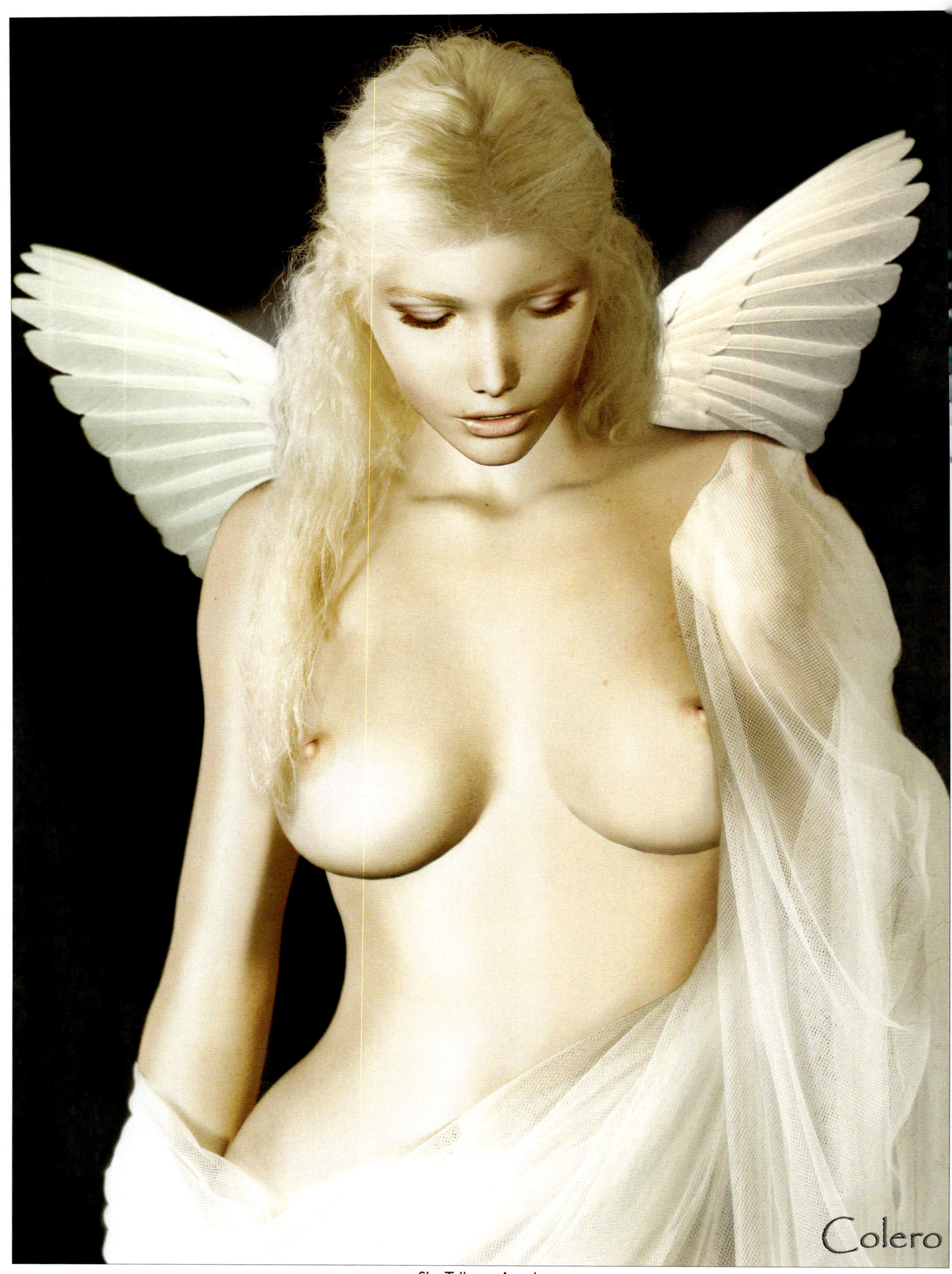

She Talks to Angels

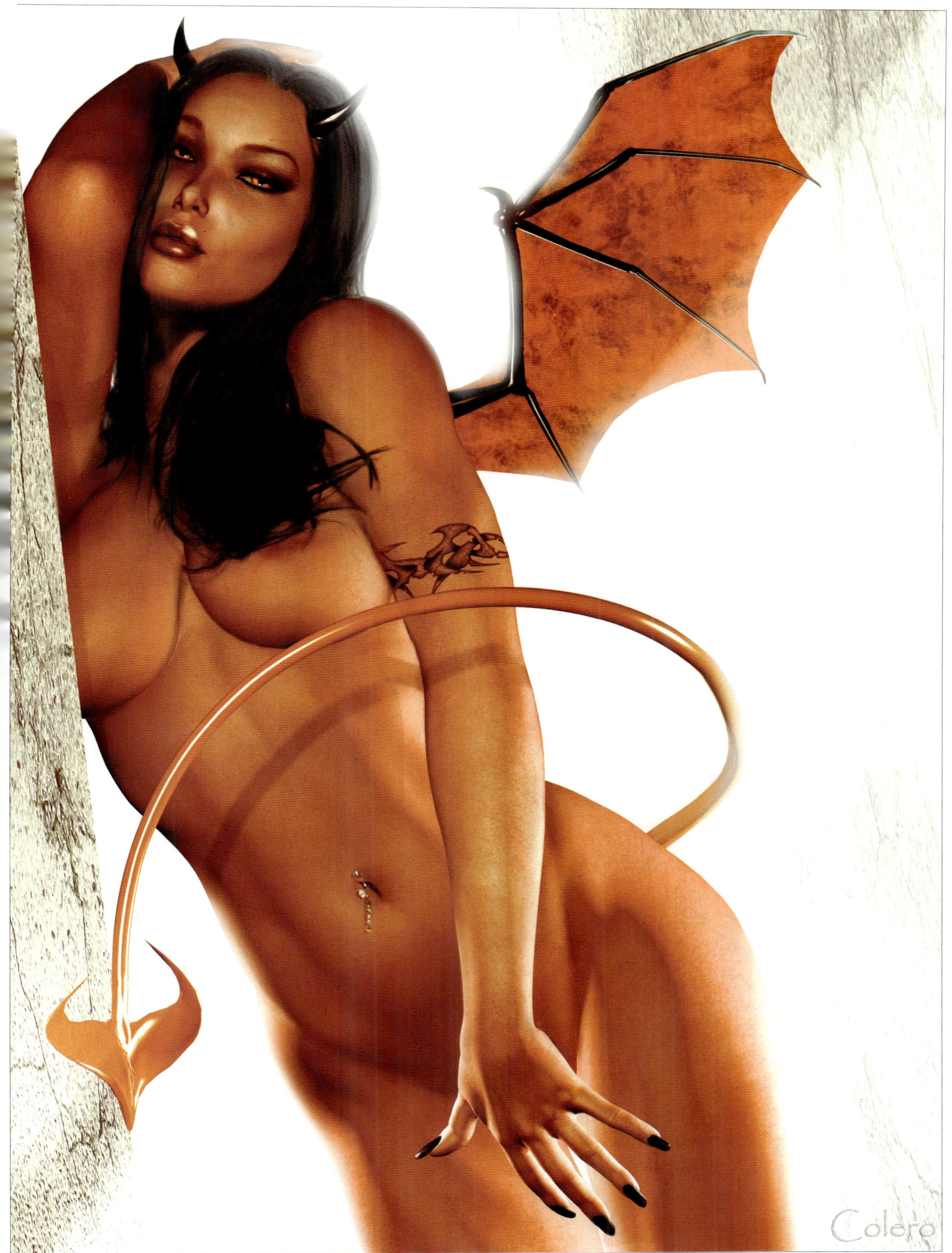

Batwing

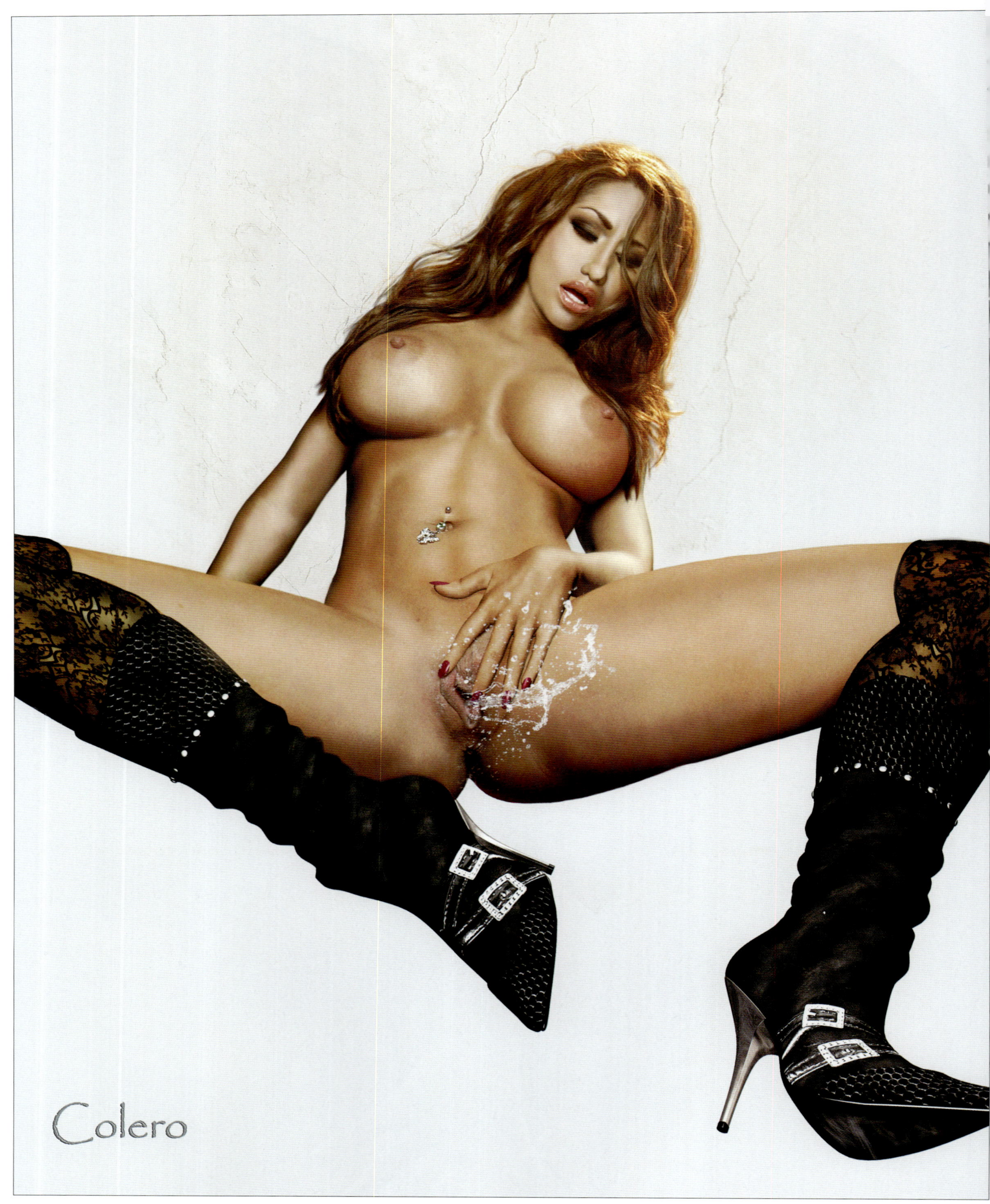
Colero

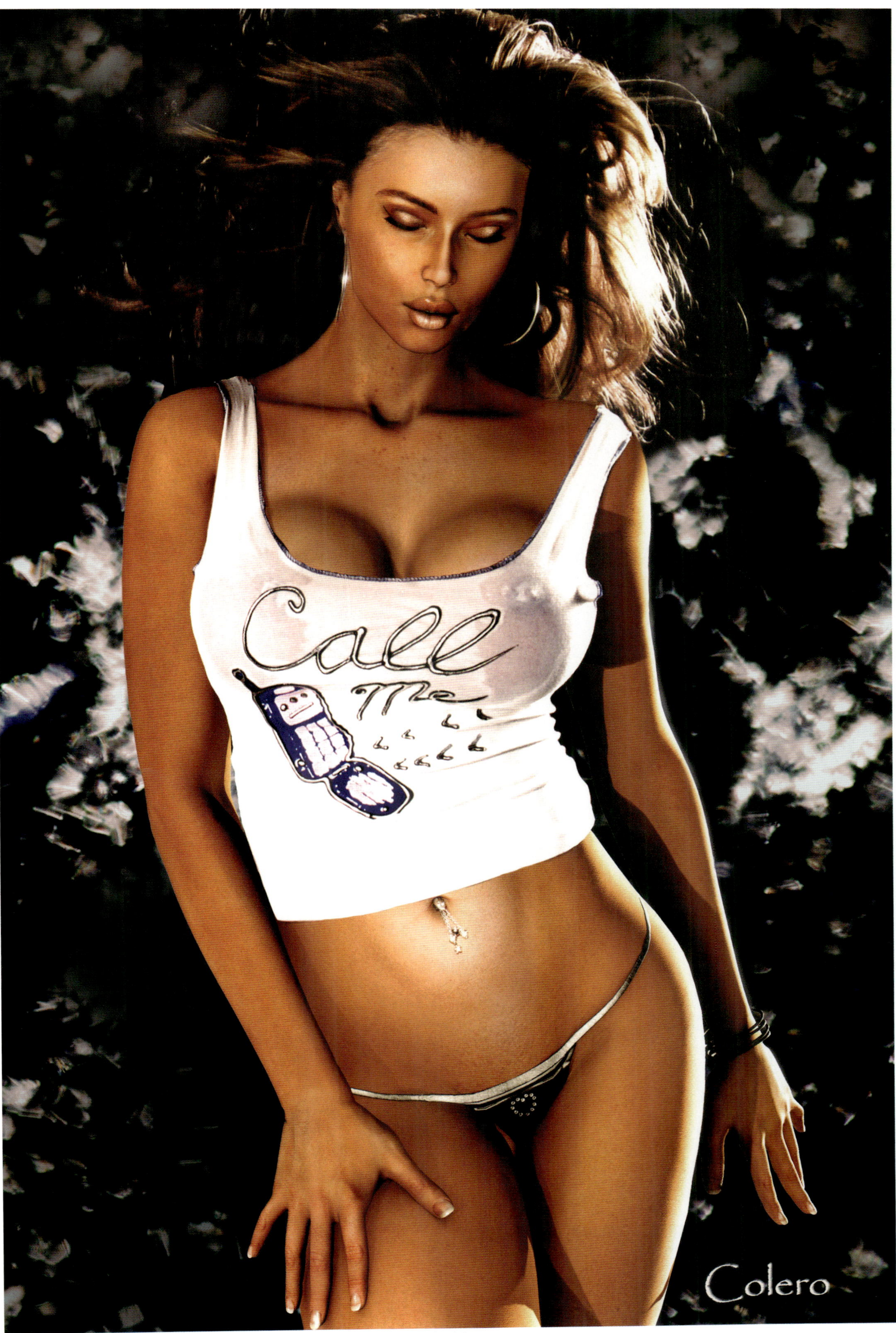

Voulez Vous

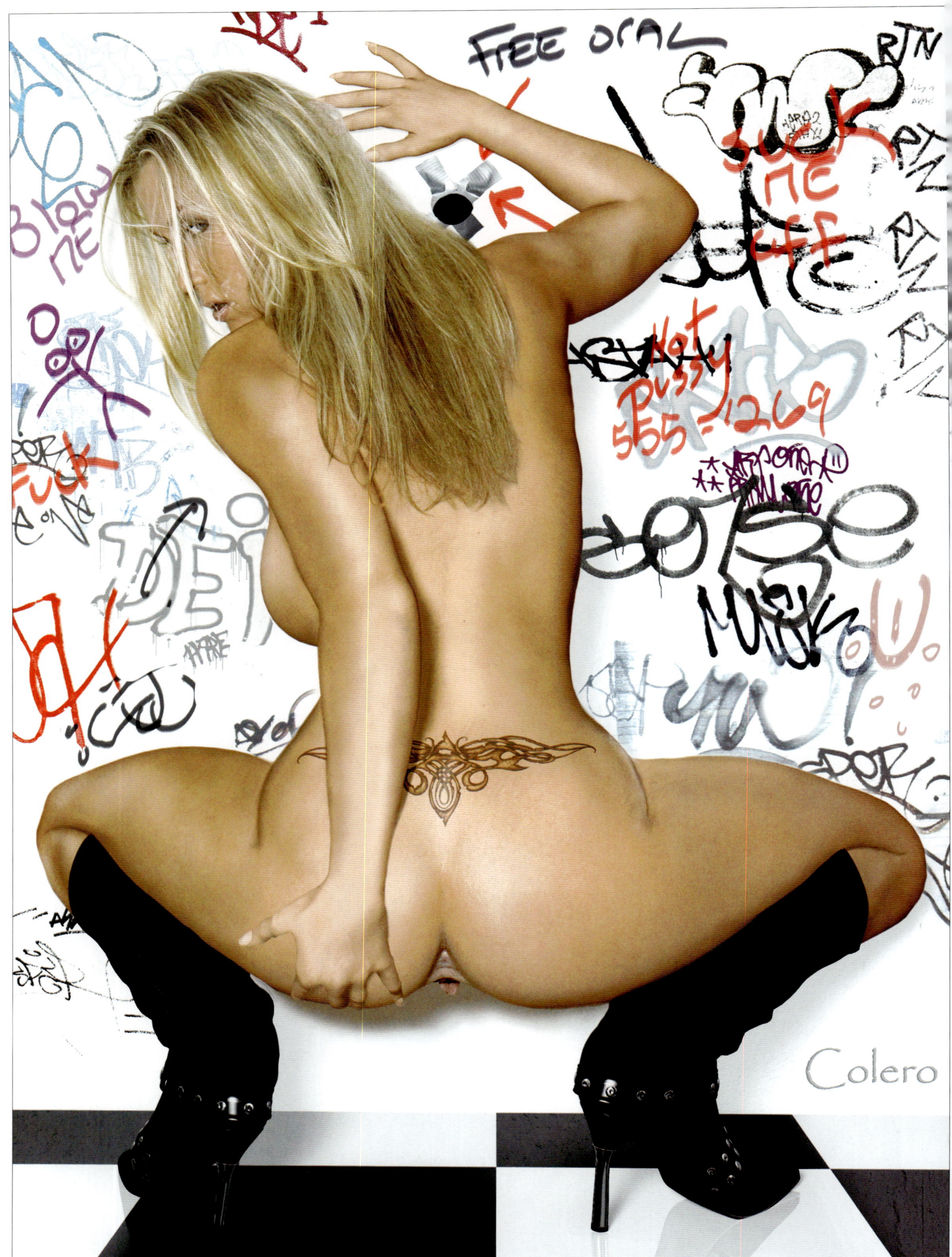

Glory Hole

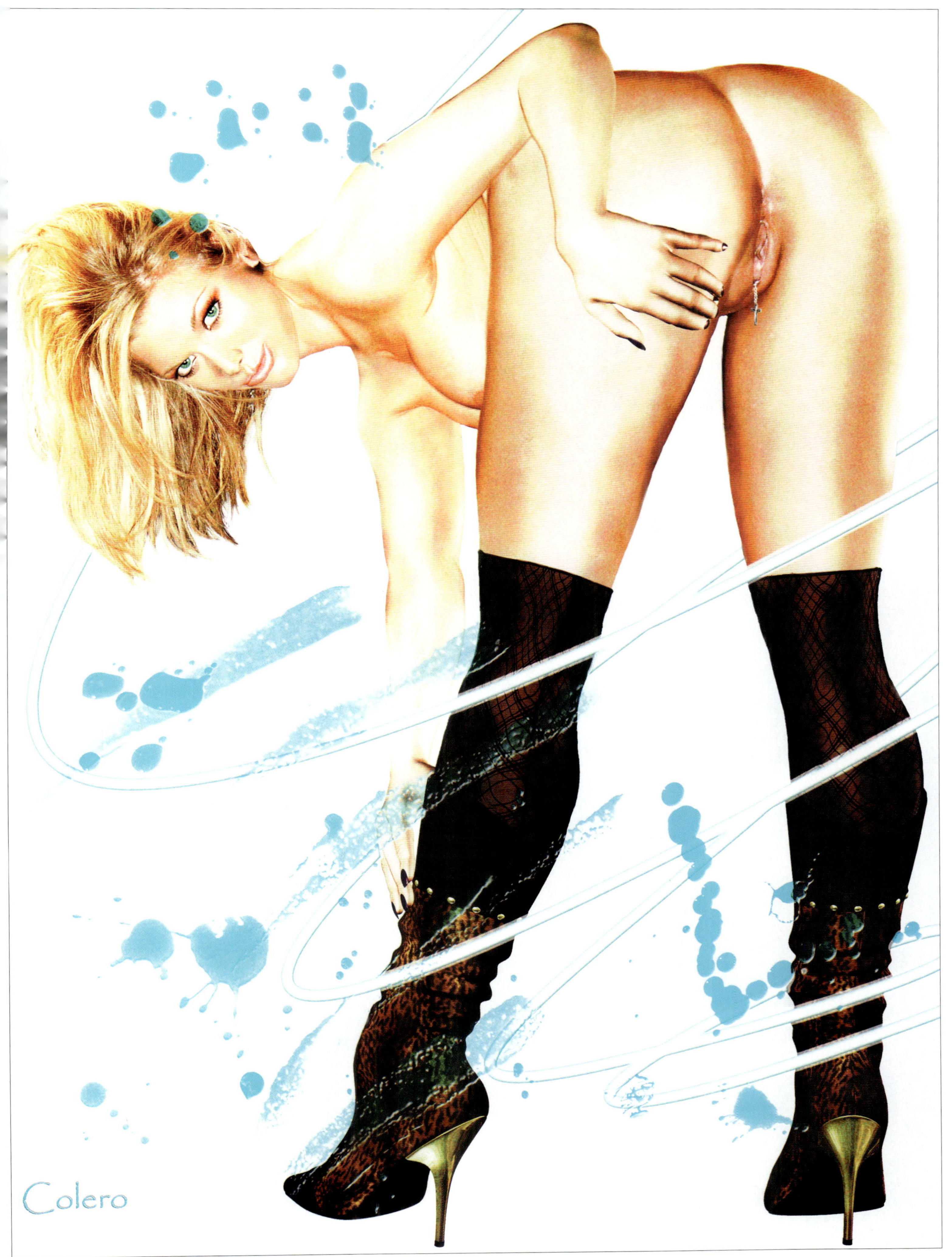

Strutter

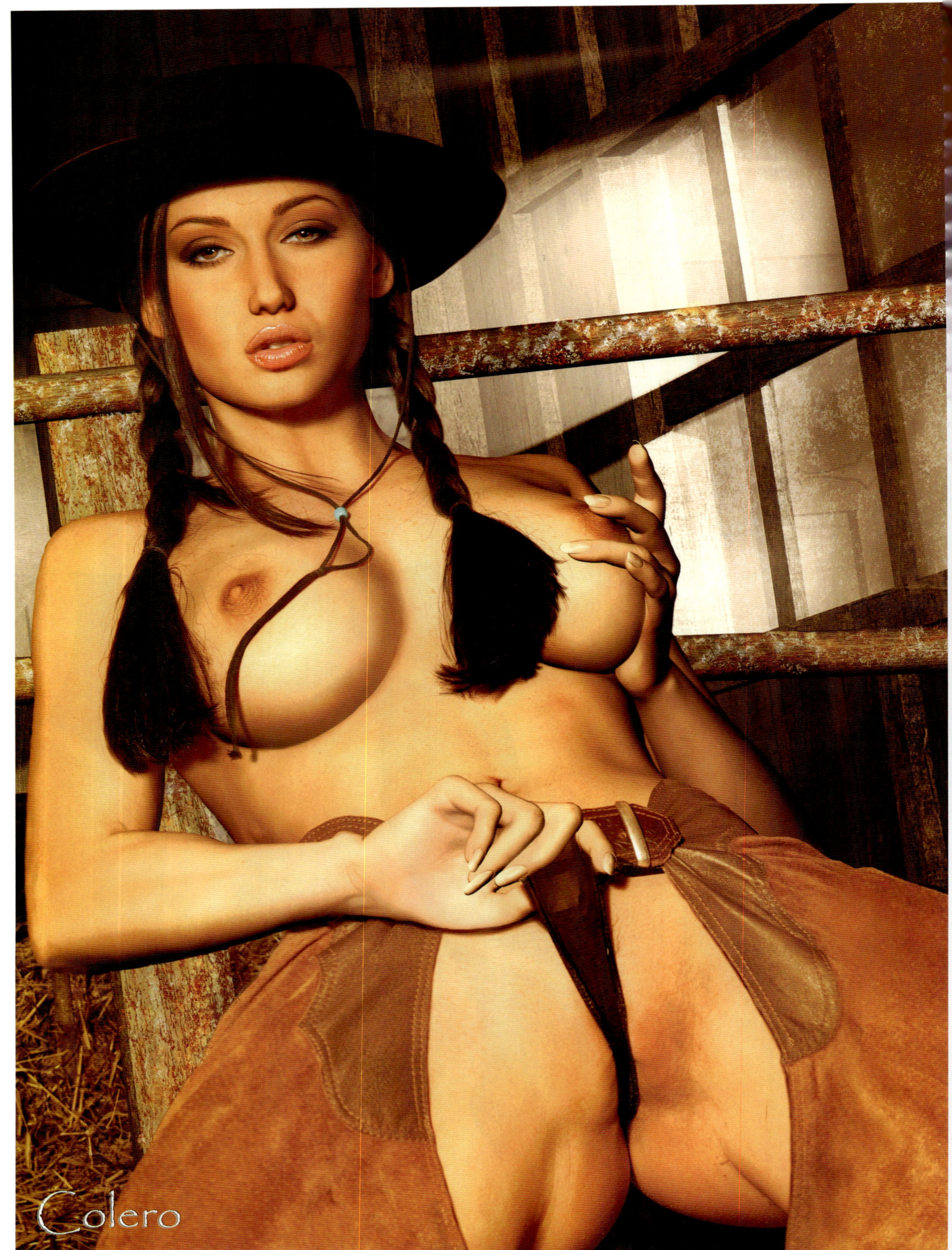

Jezebel

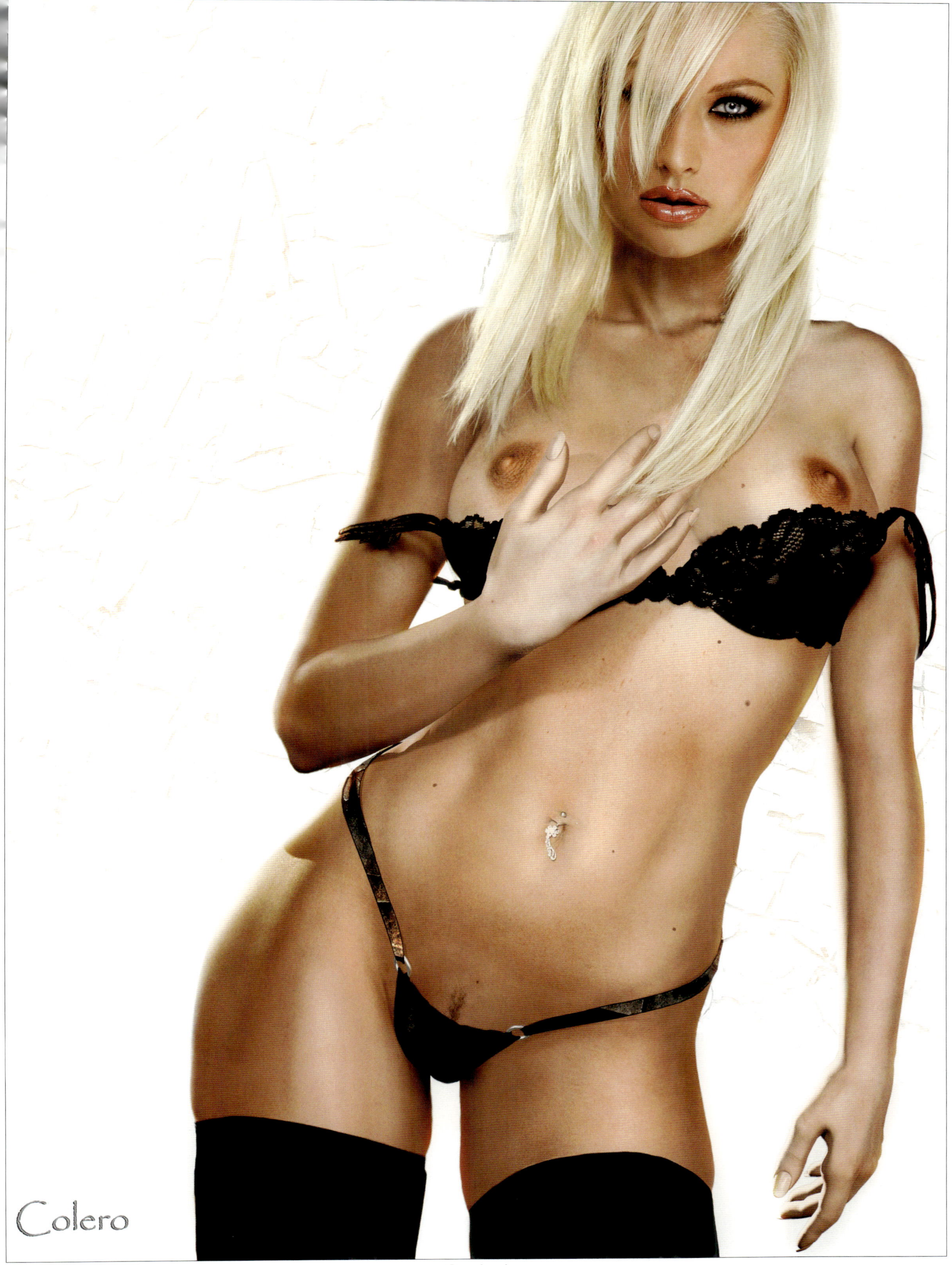

Overload

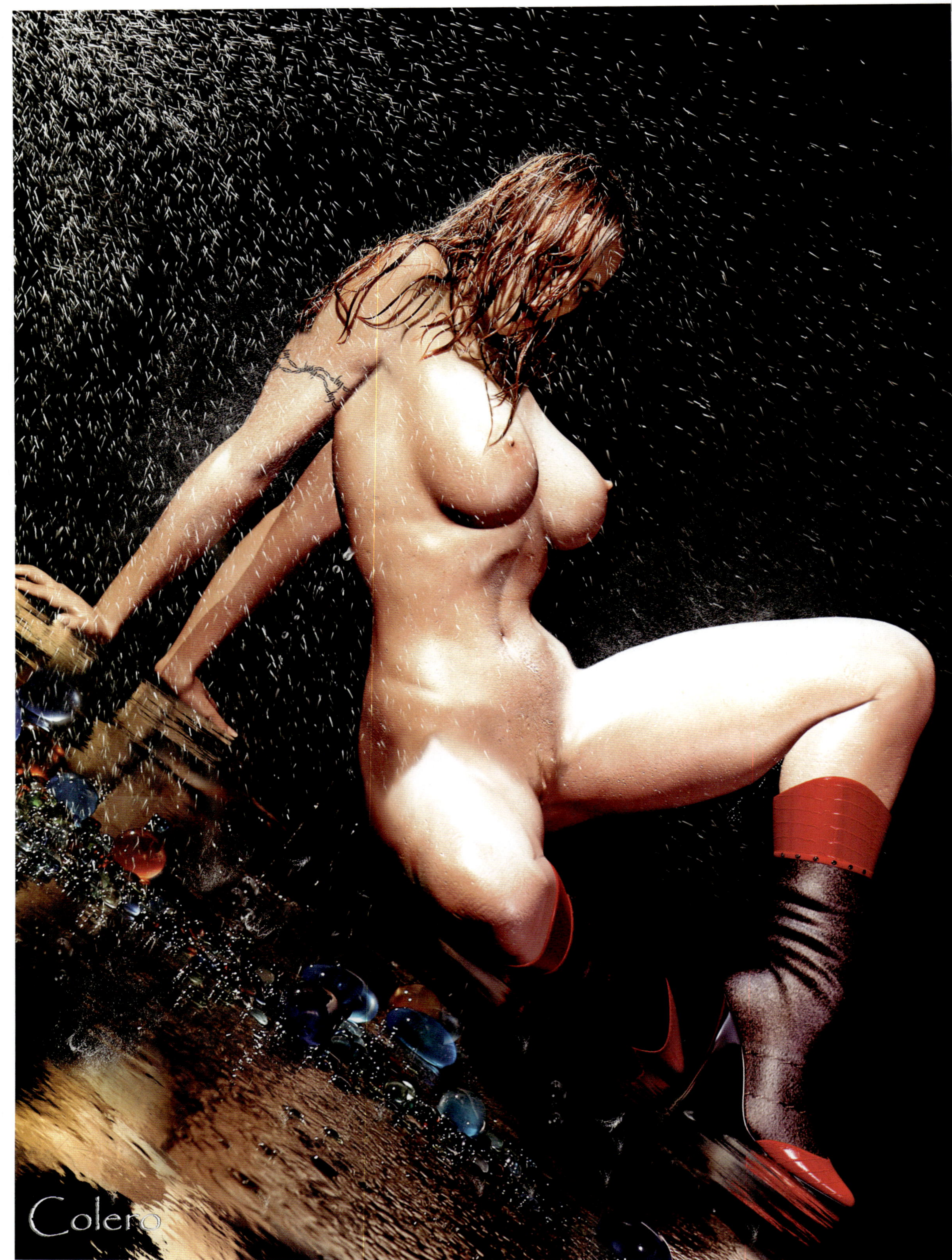

Eau

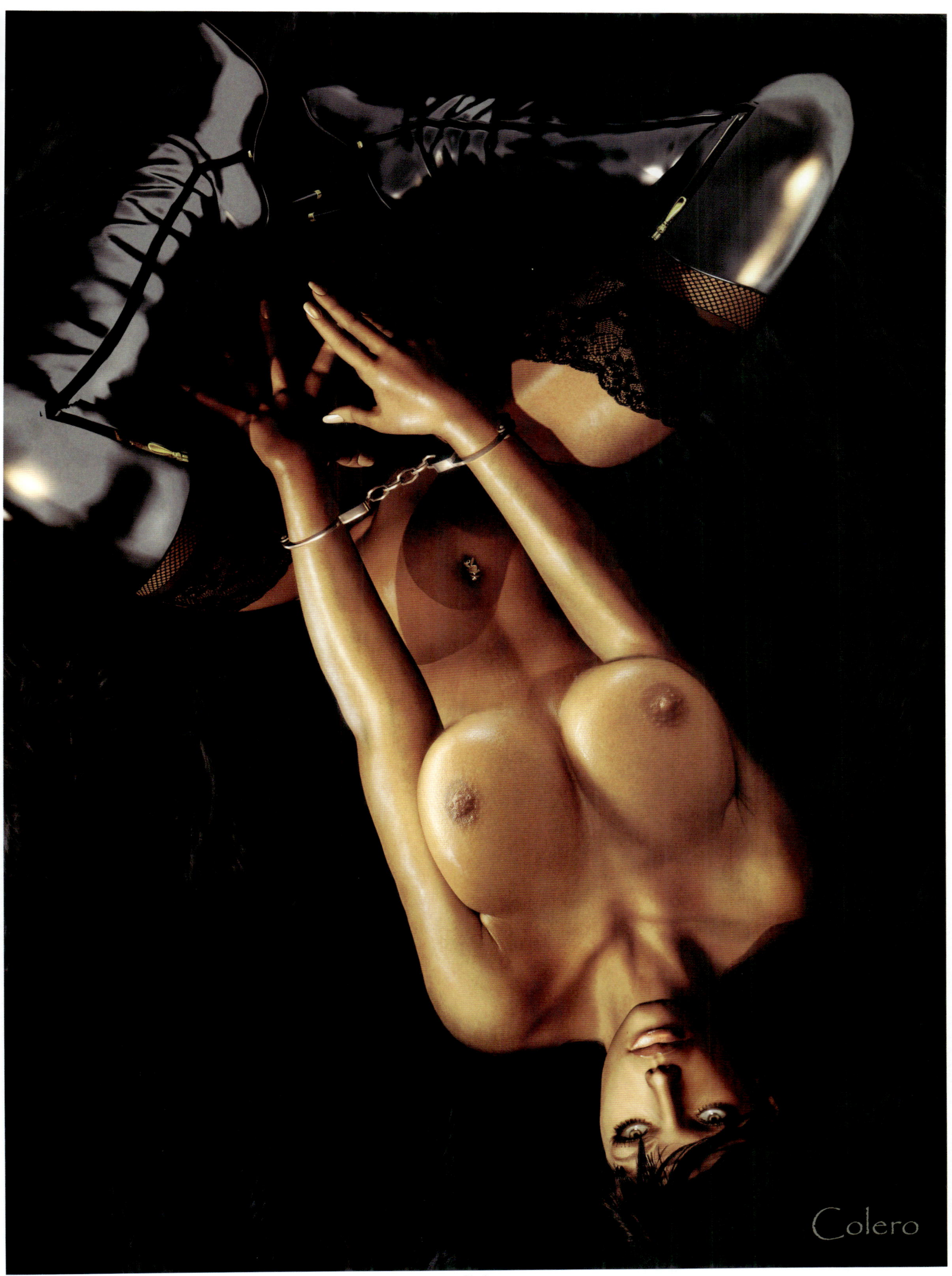

Slick

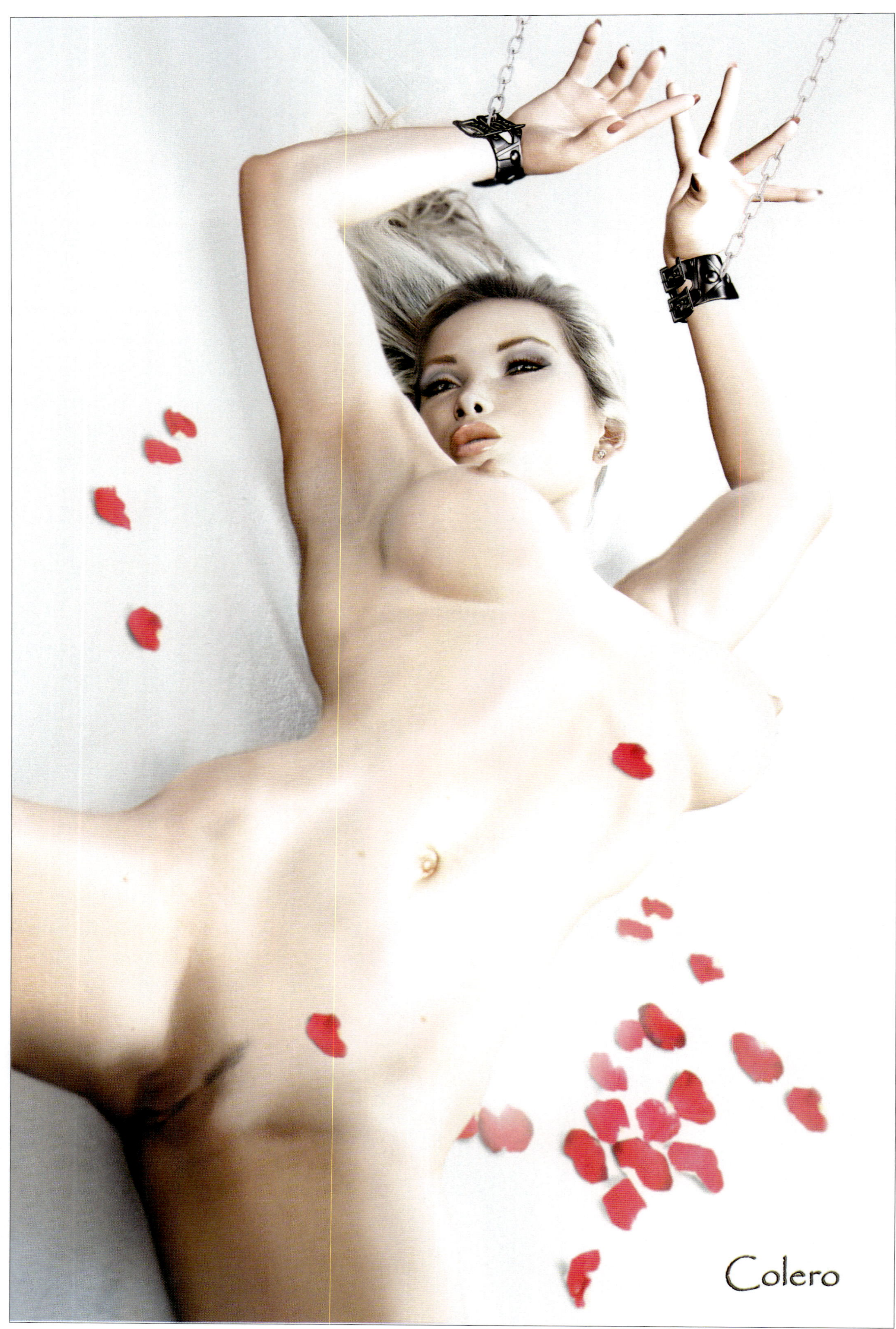

An Easier Affair

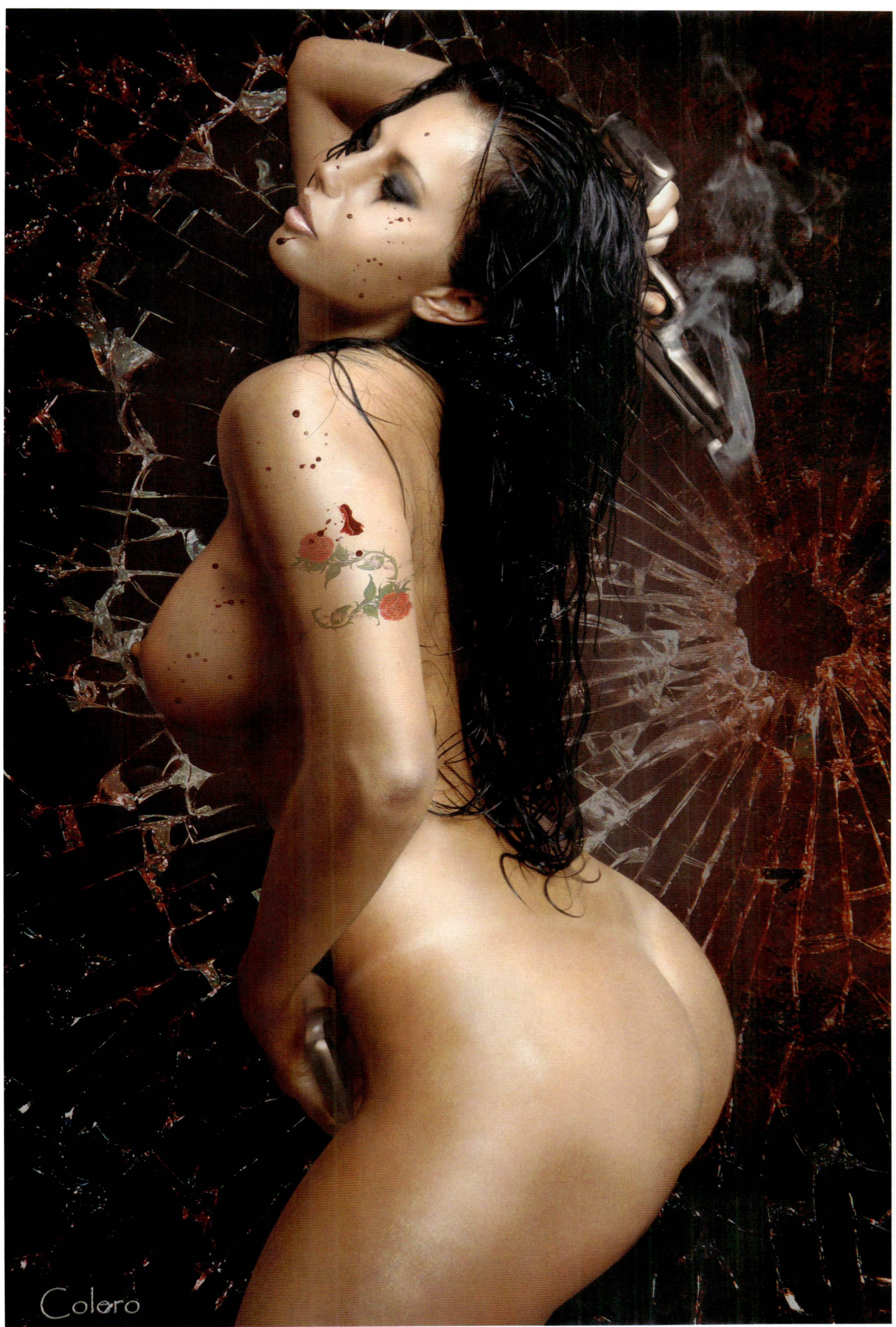

Guns n' Roses

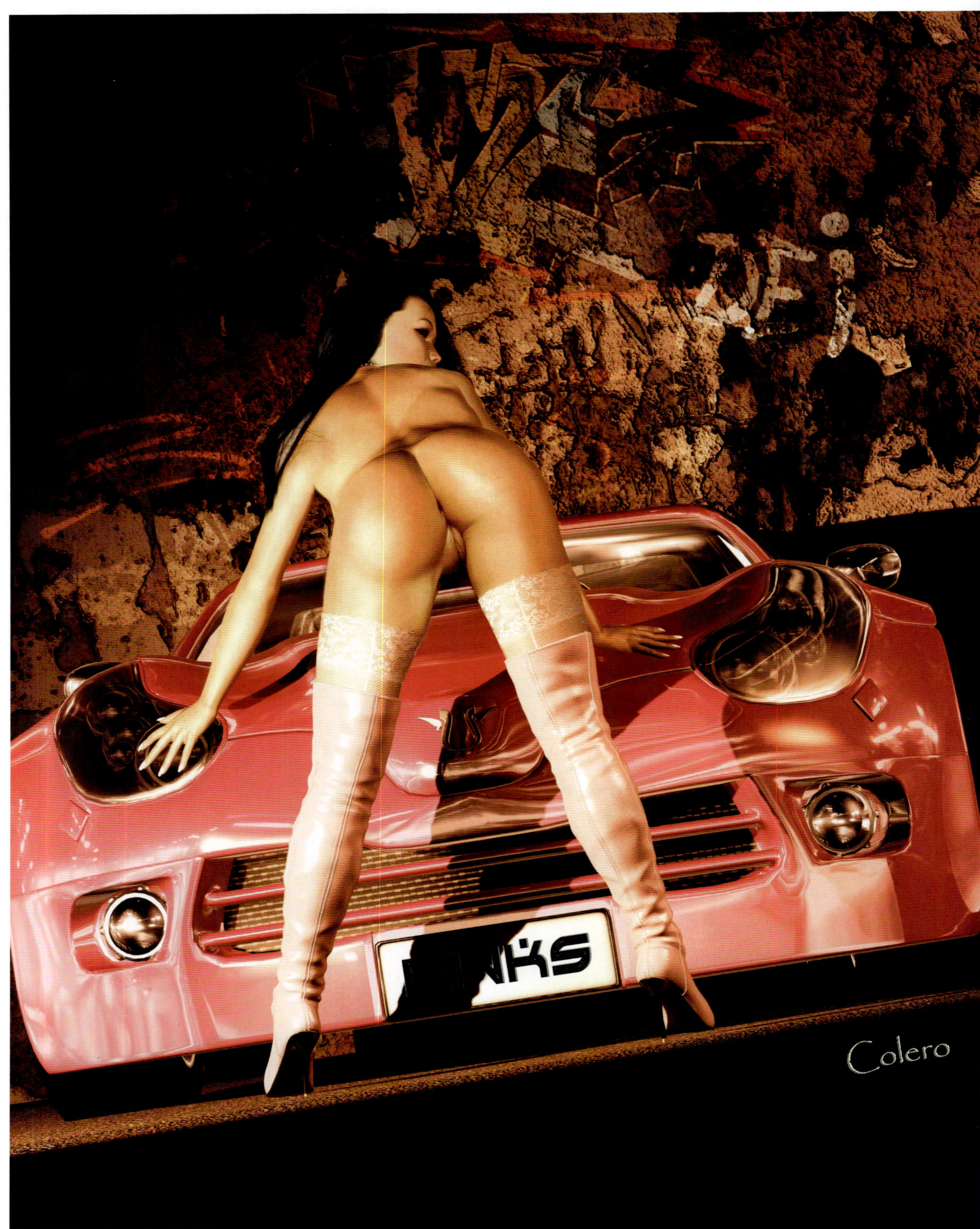

Pinks

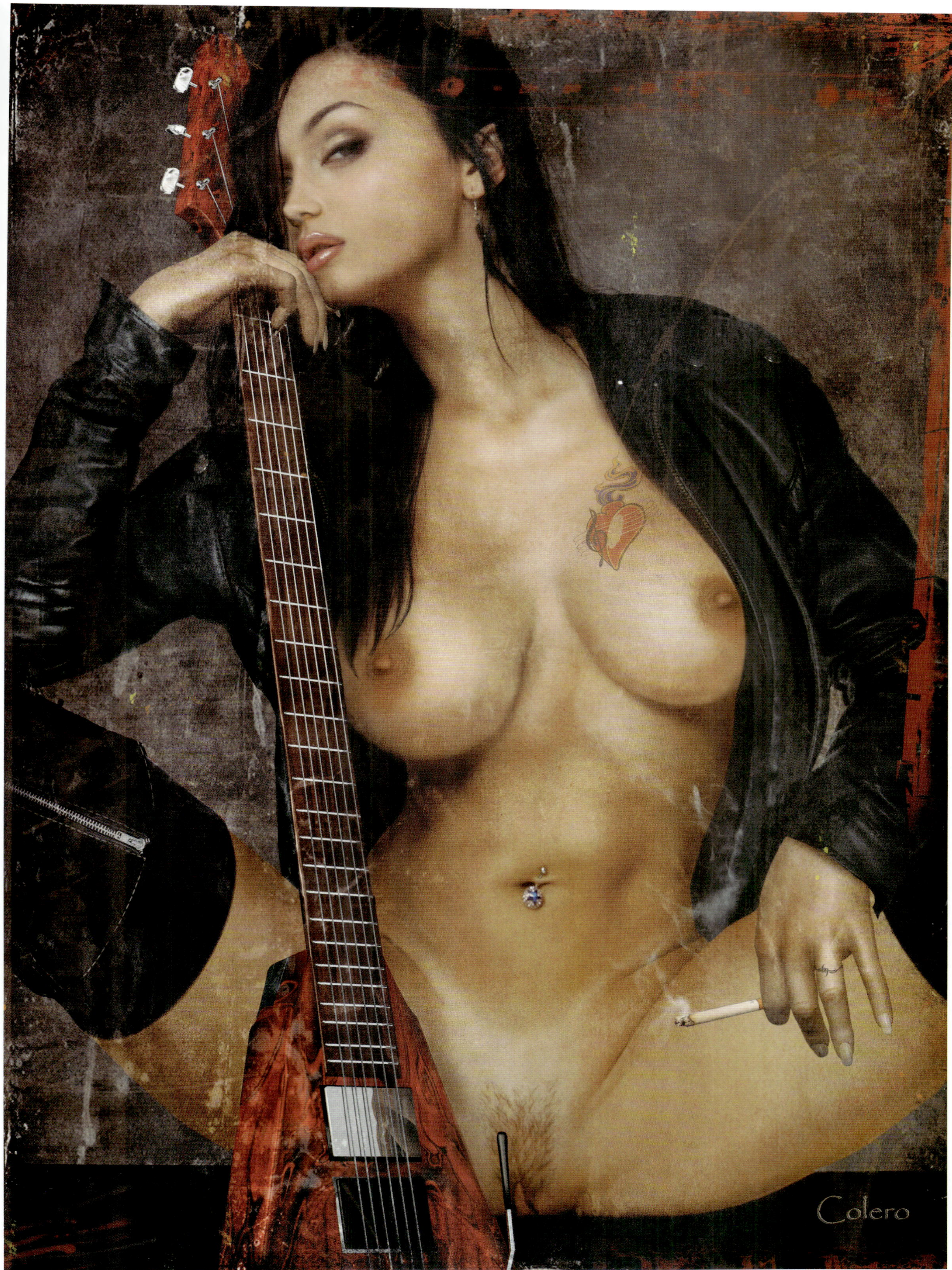

Rockstar

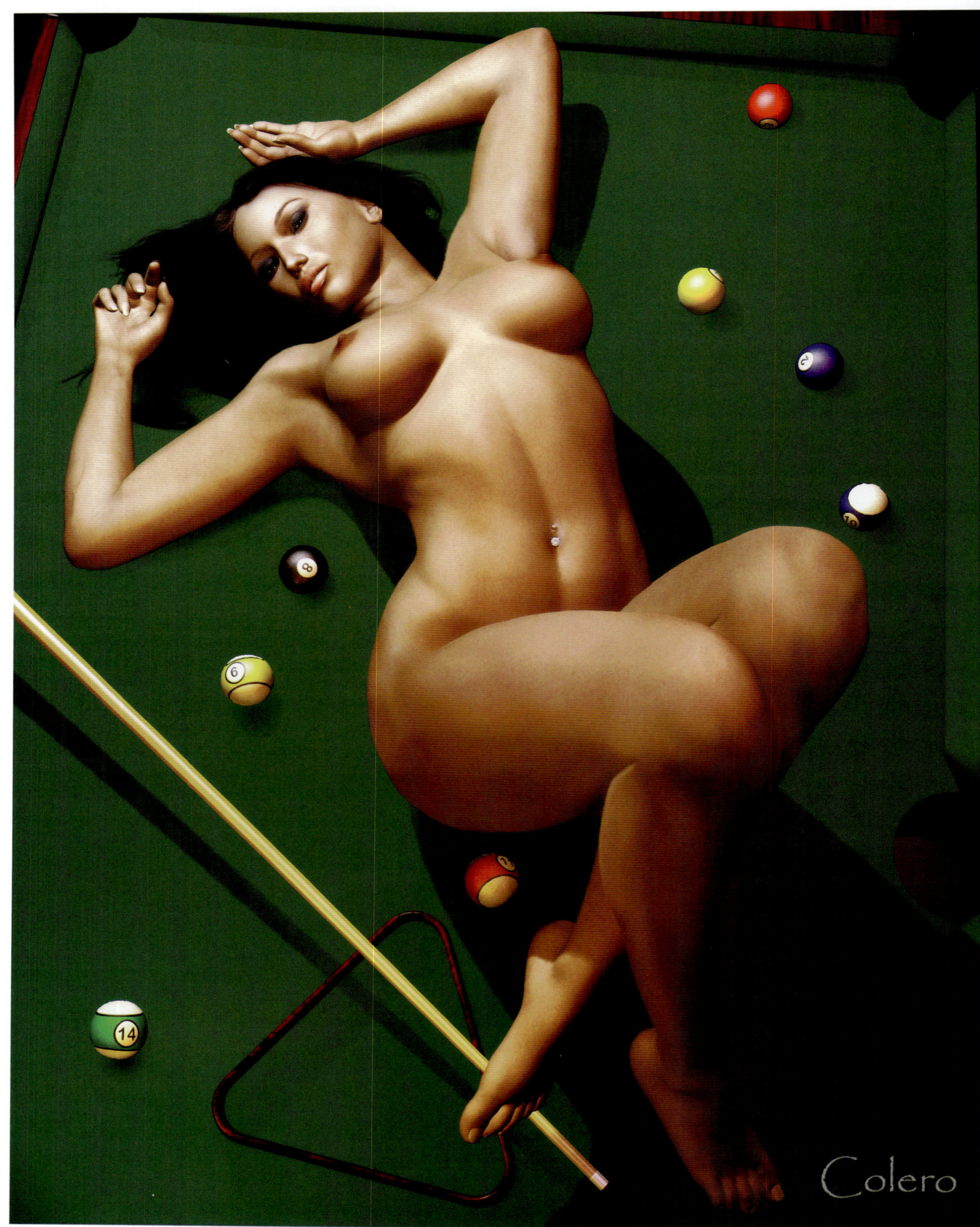

The Hustler

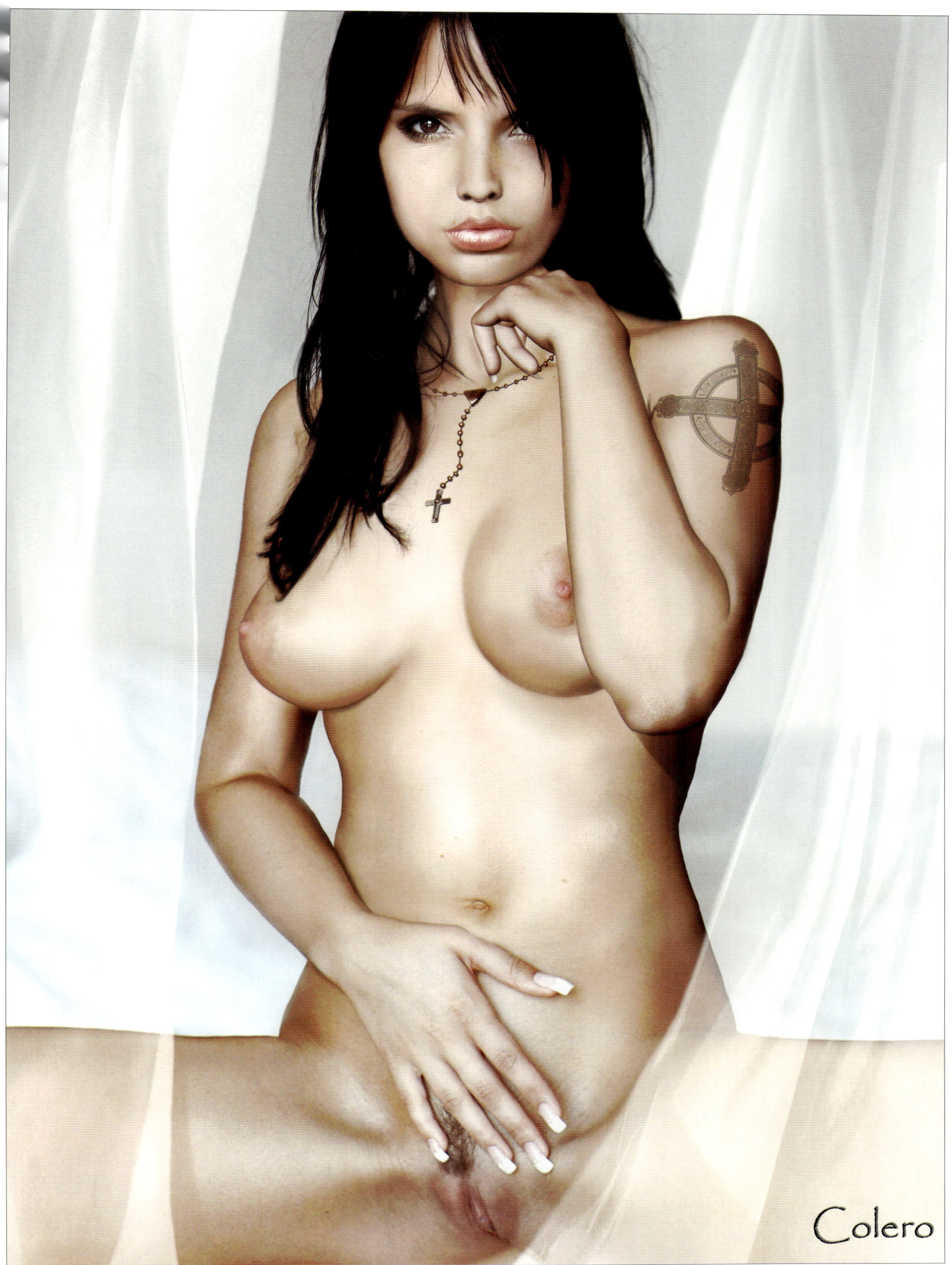

Magdelena

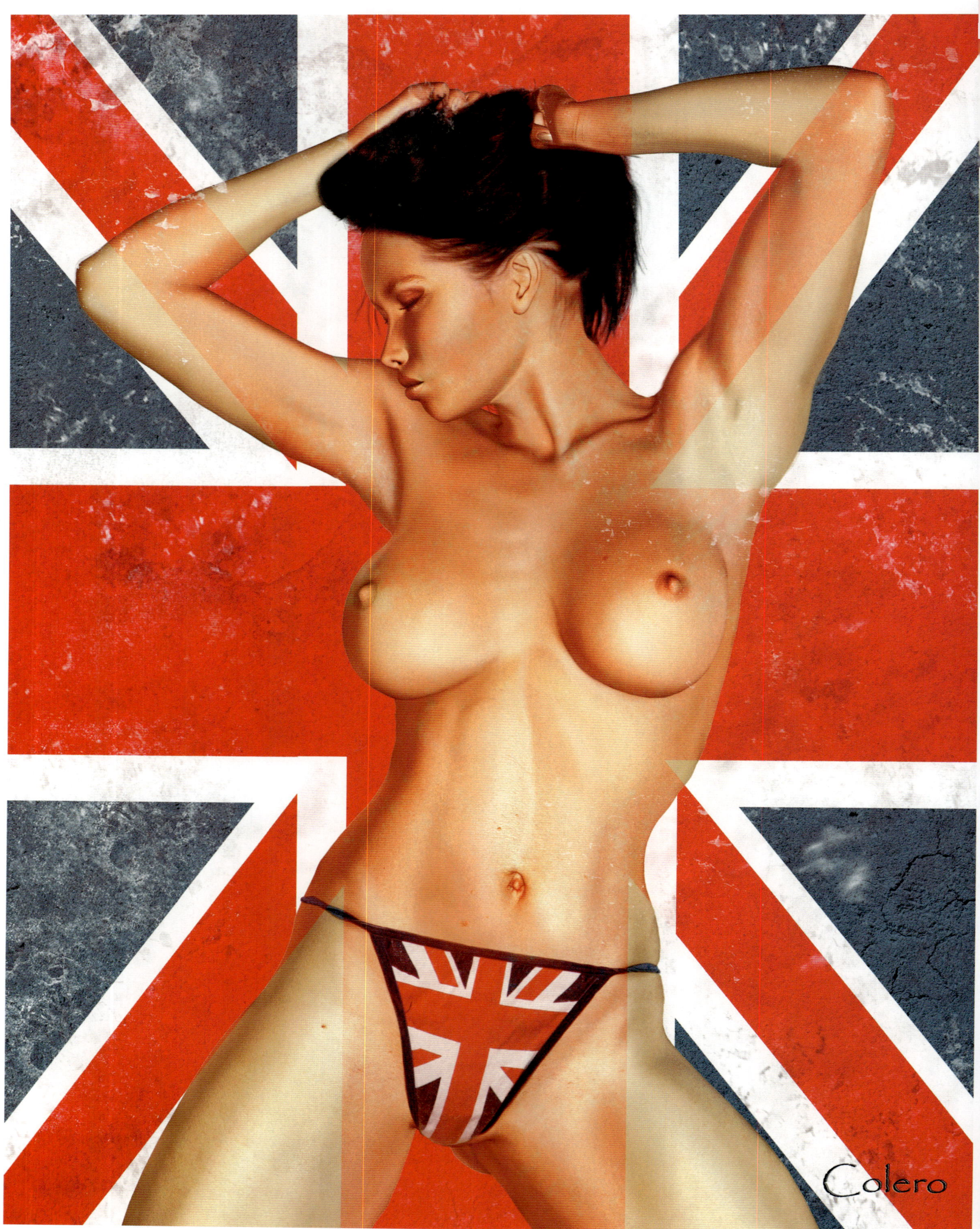

London Calling

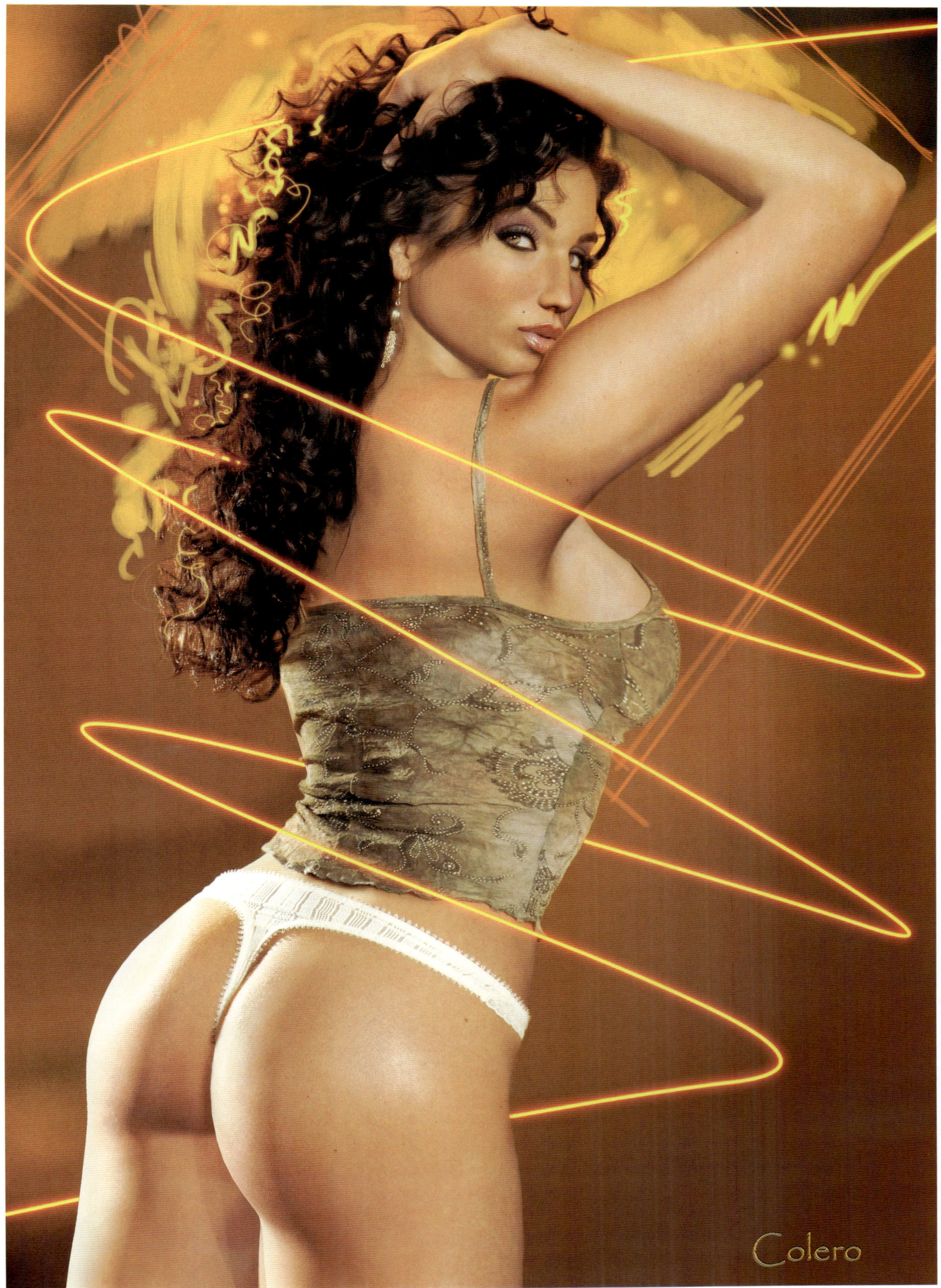

Cracklin' Rosie

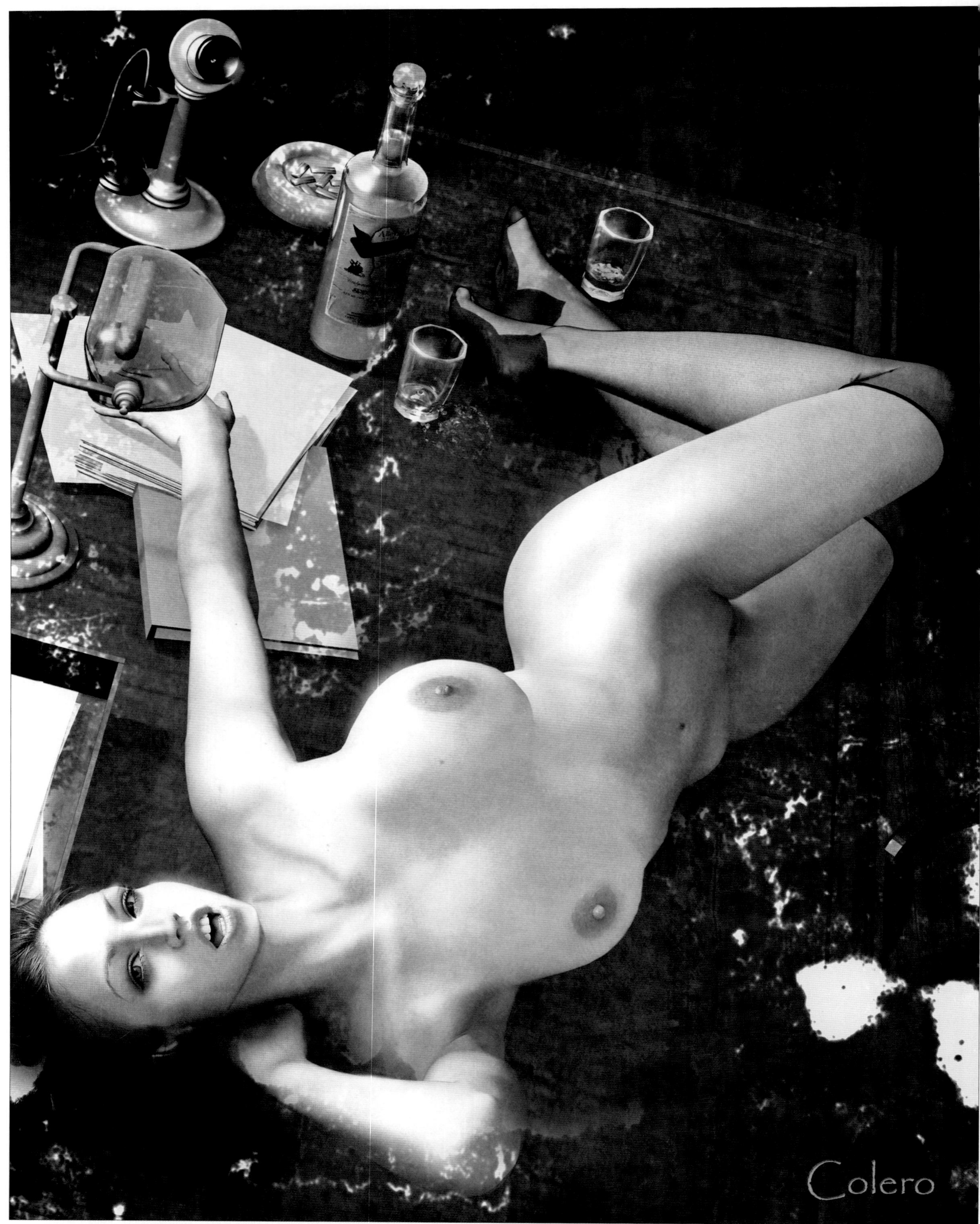

Femme Fatale

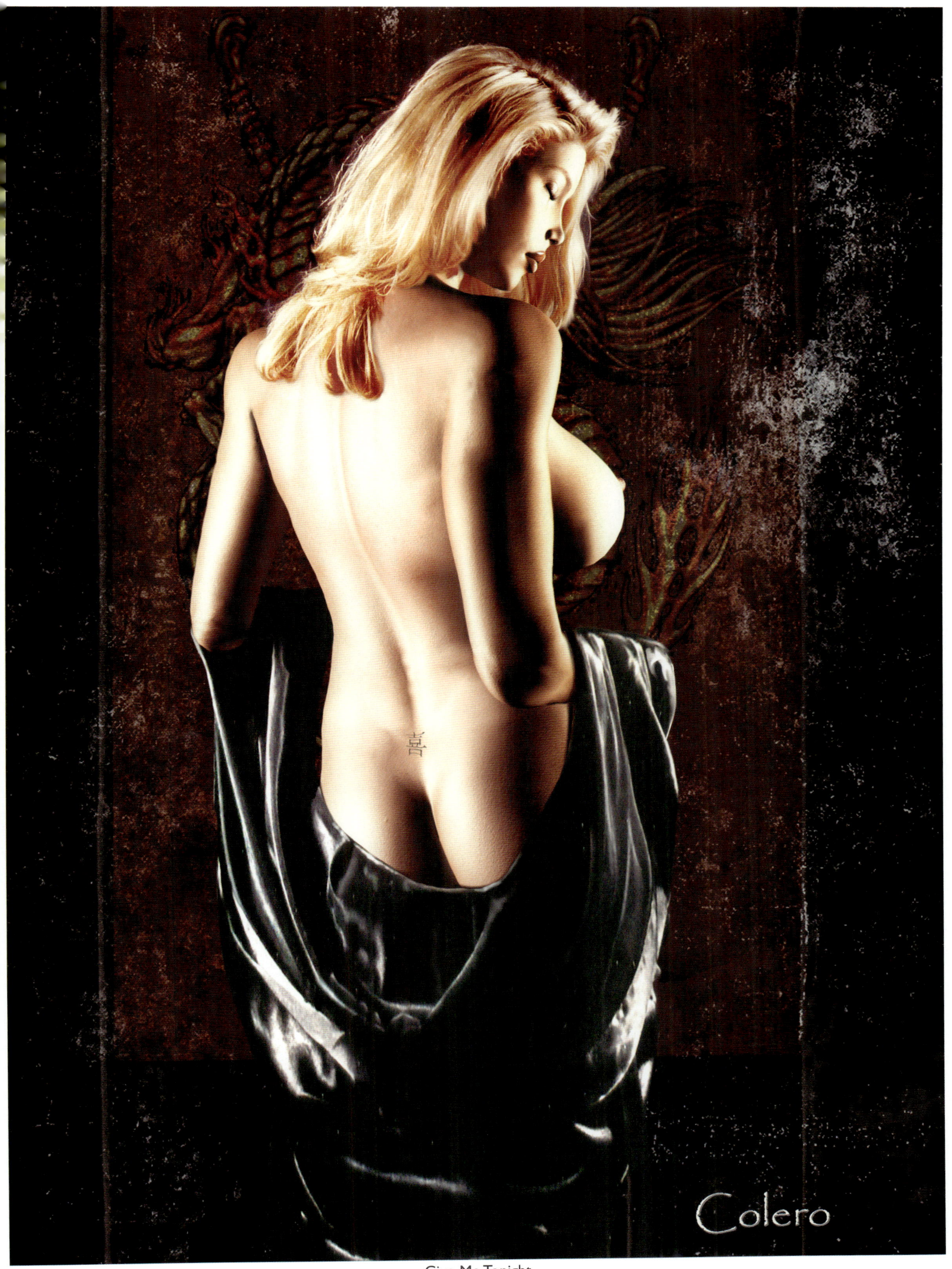

Give Me Tonight

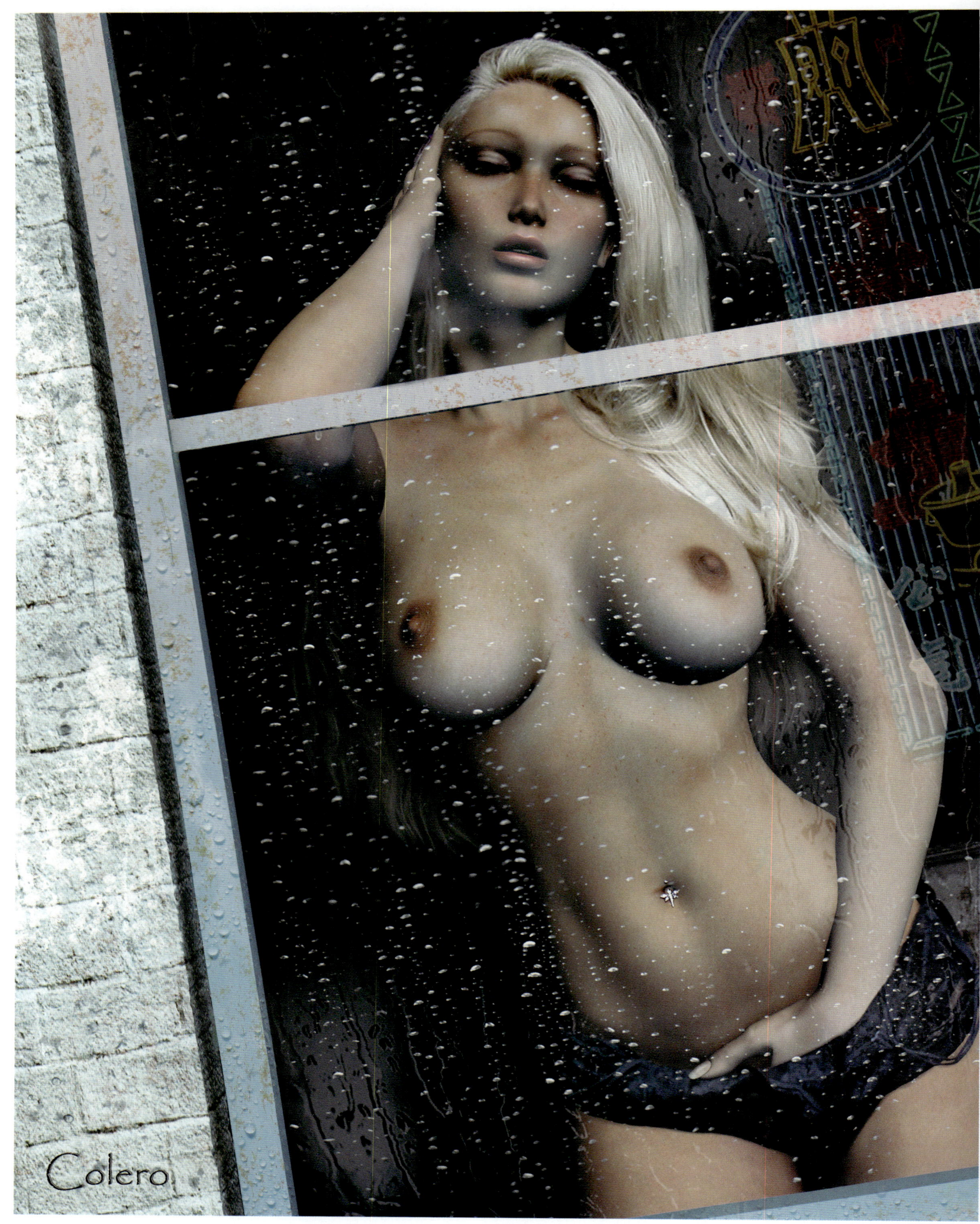

That's Where You Find Love

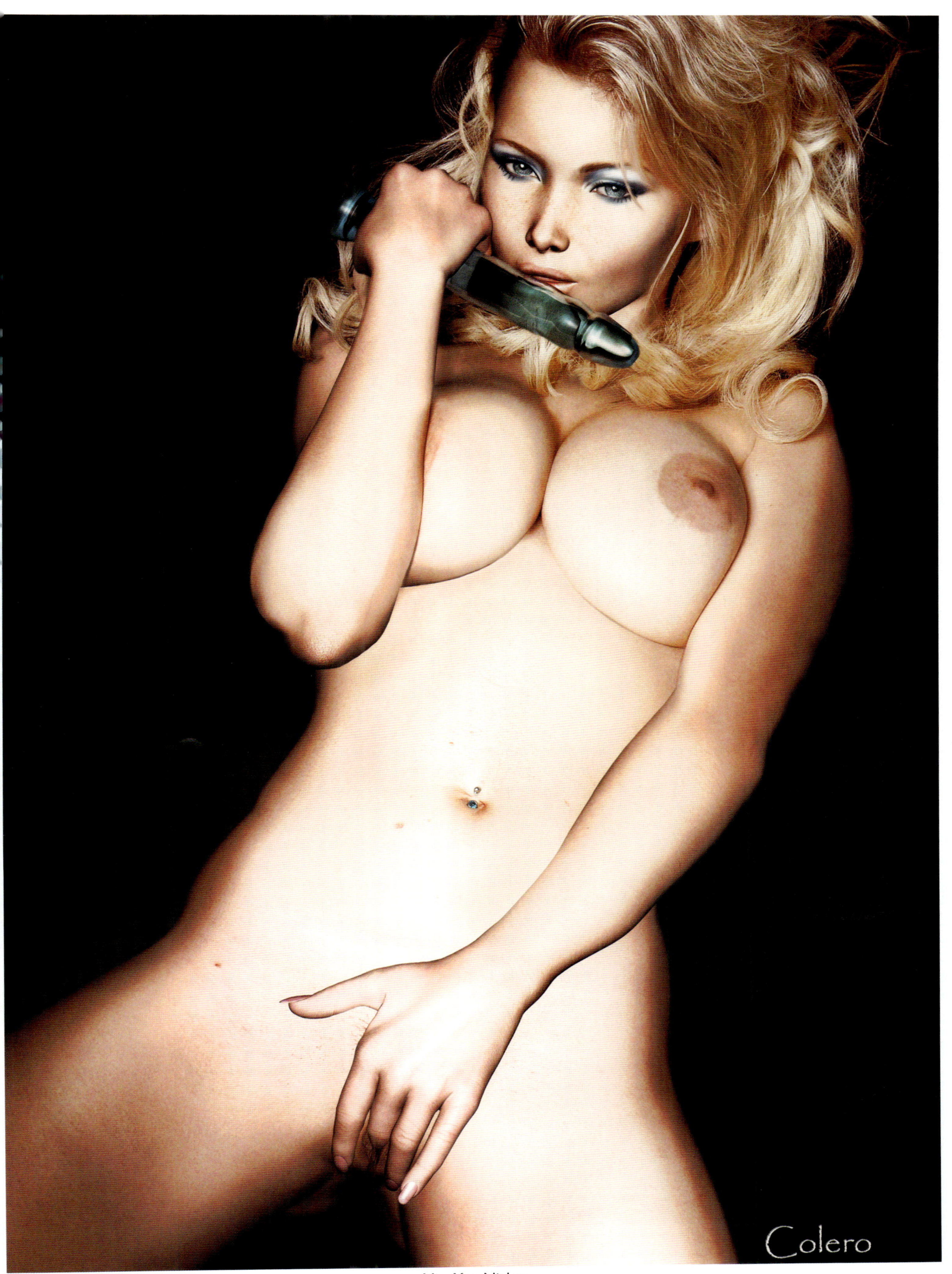

Miss You Nights

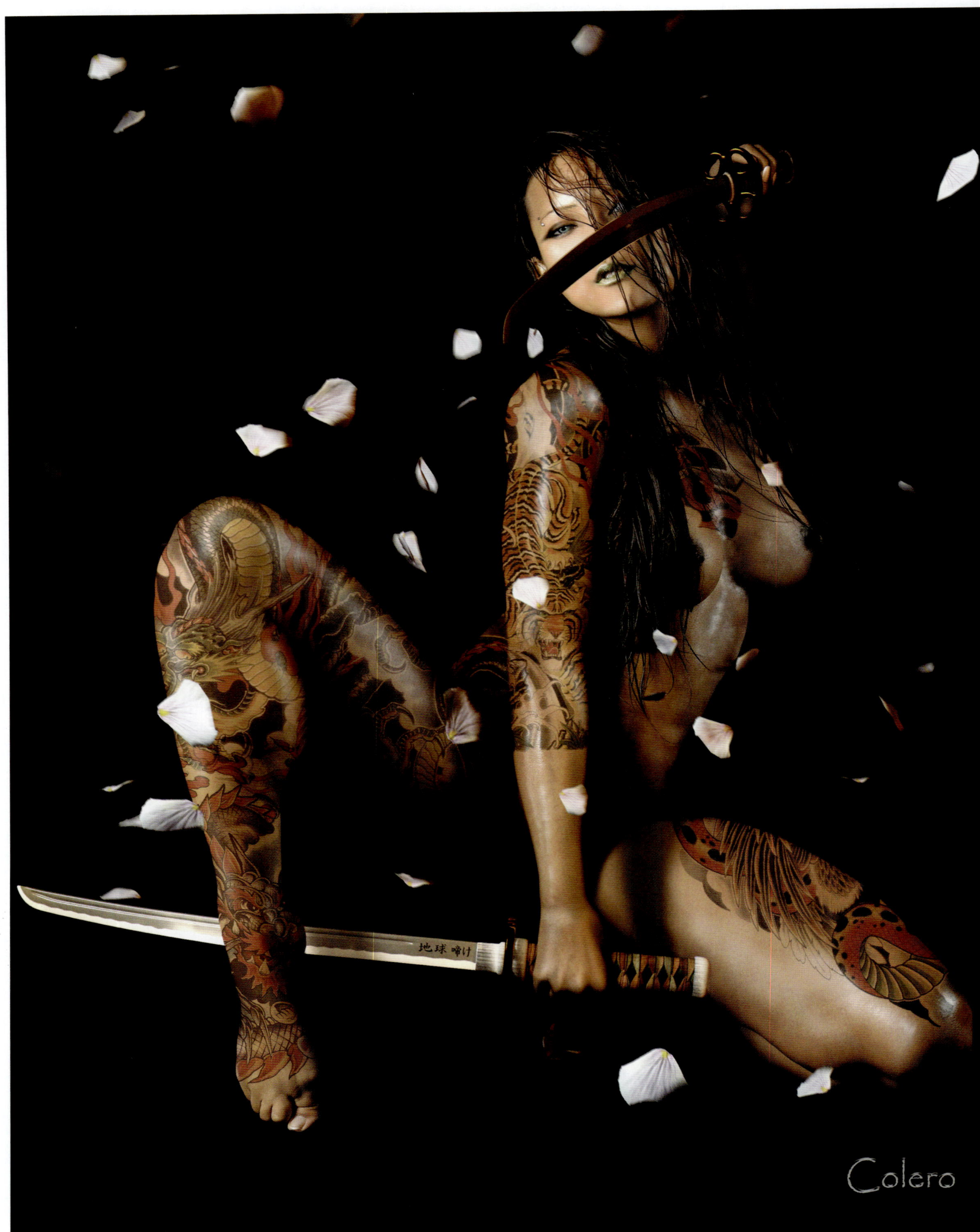

Without Guilt or Sin

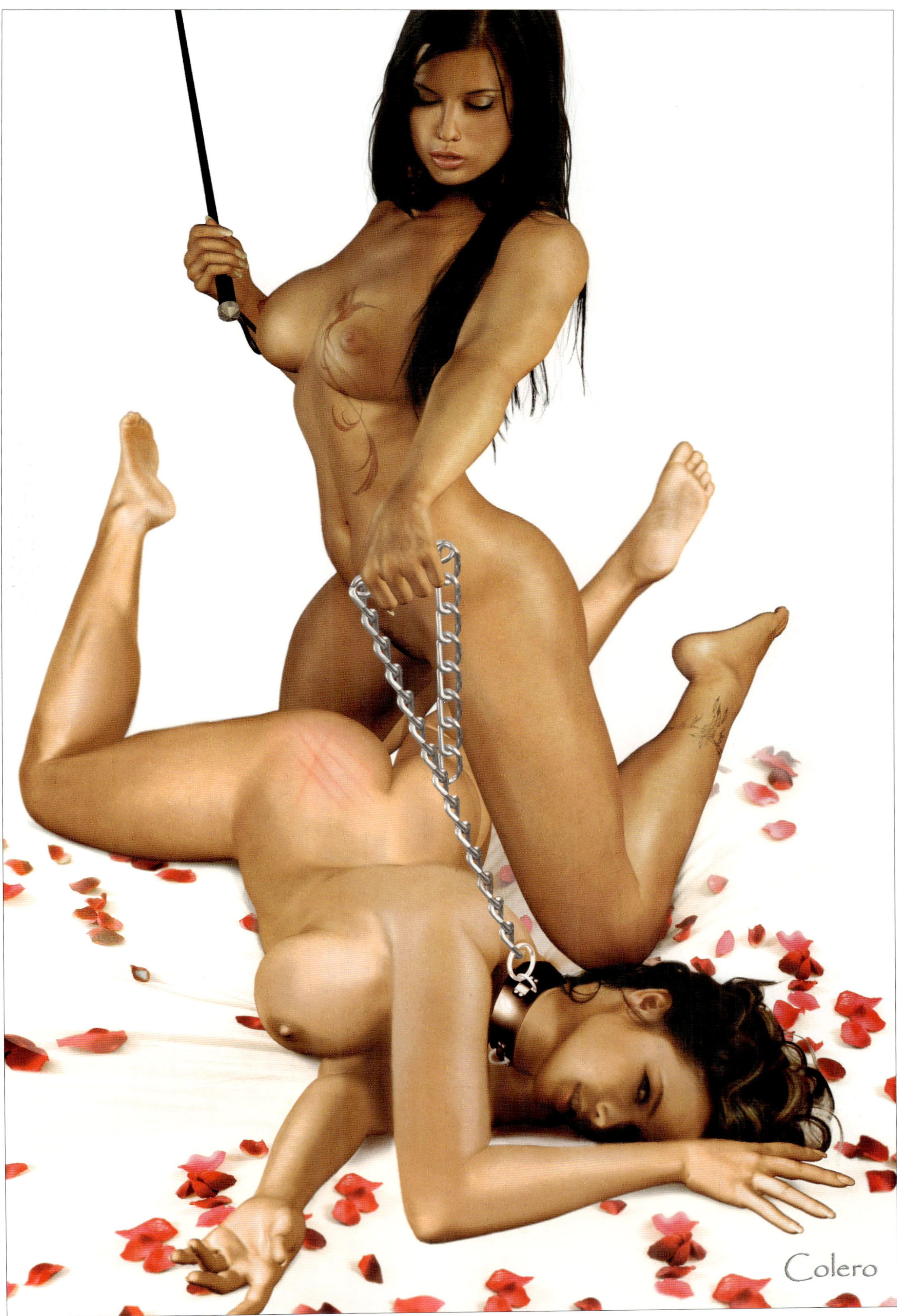

Hit Me Baby

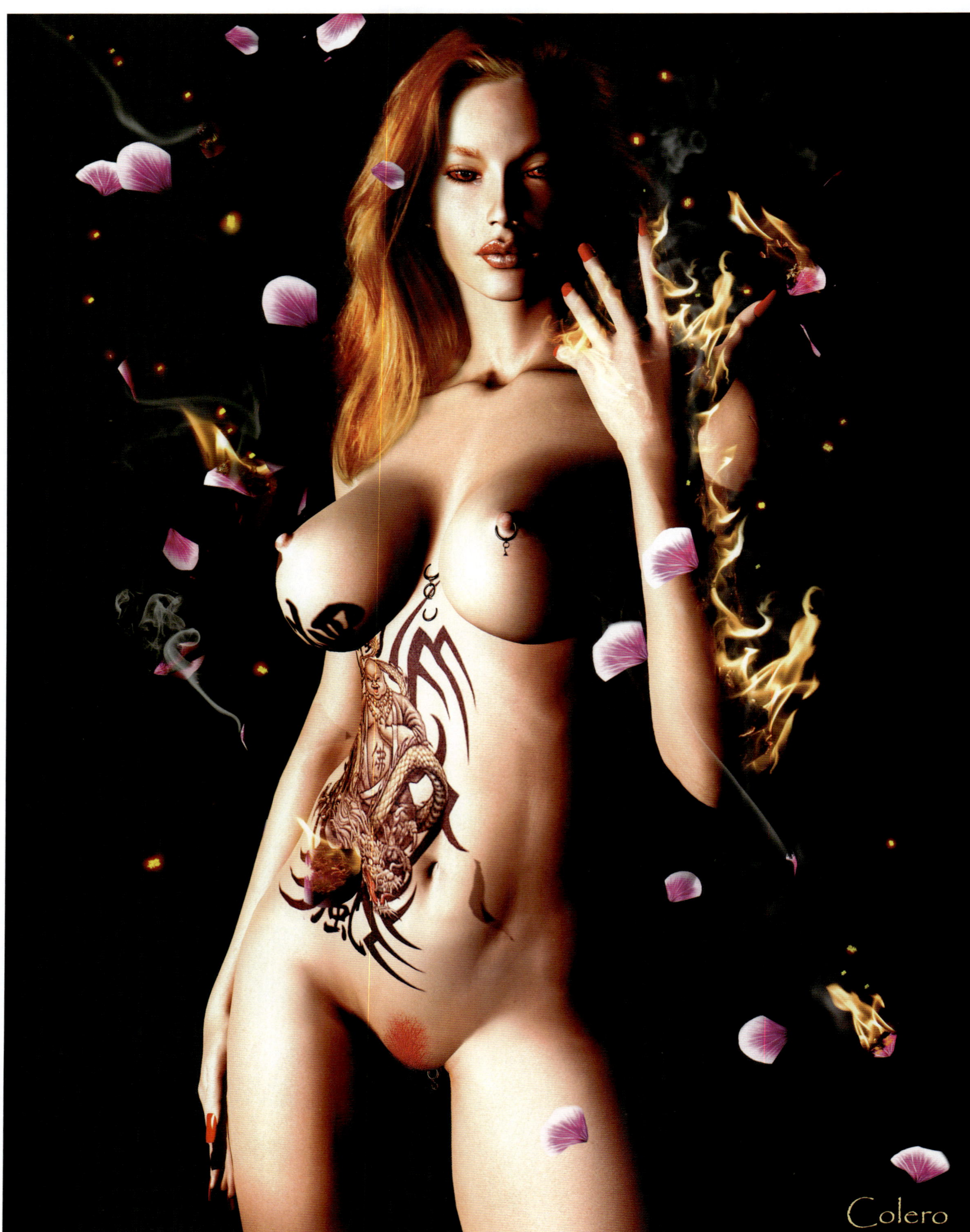

For Love We Burn

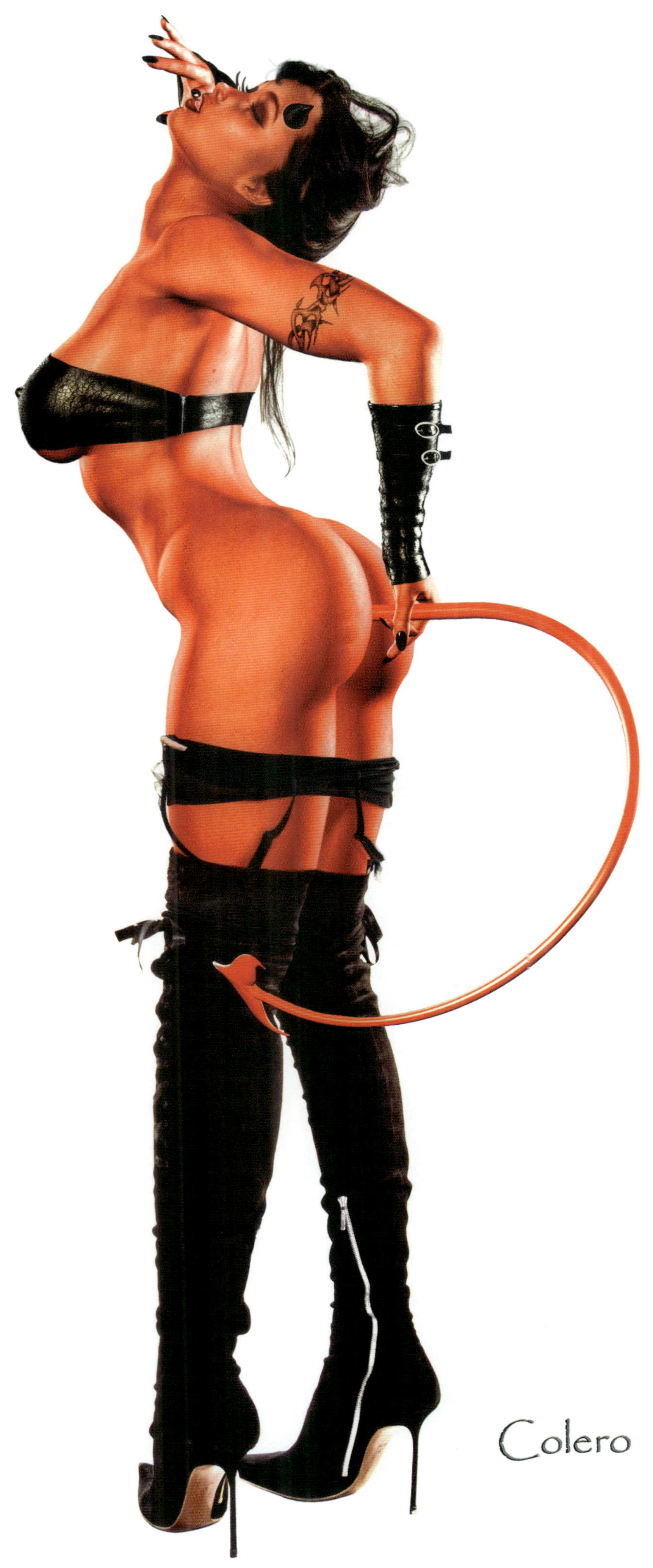

Slide It In

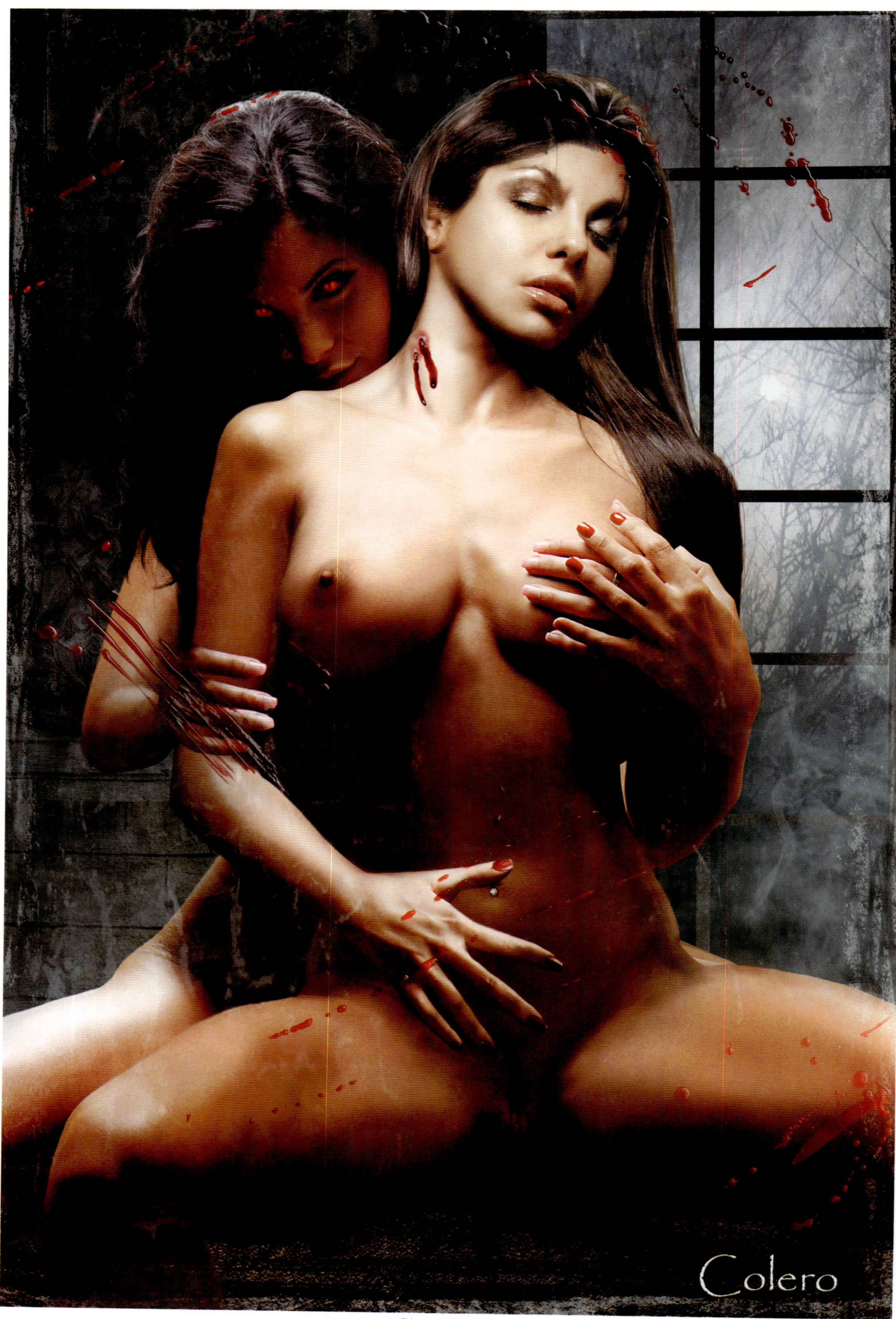

Blood Work

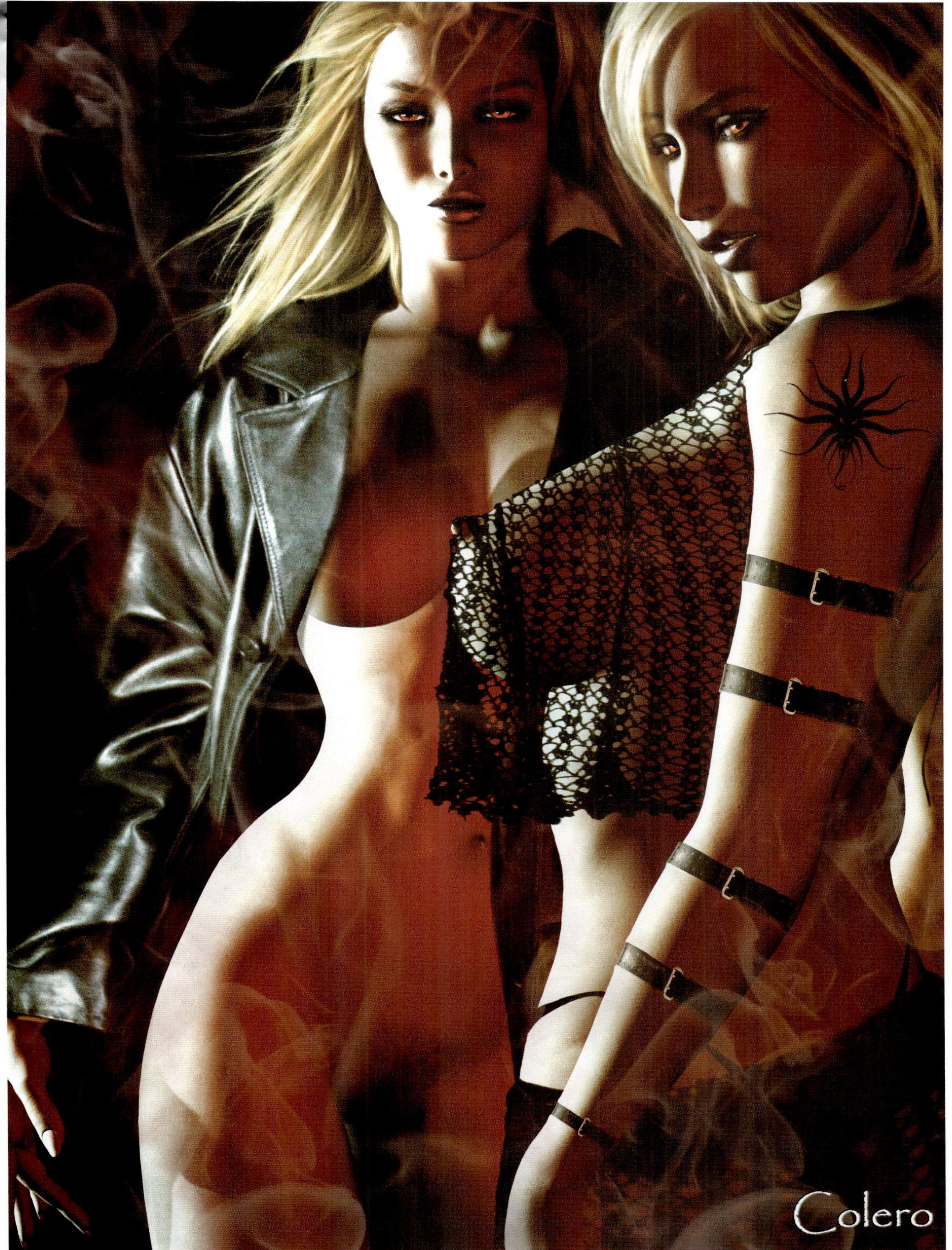

Coven

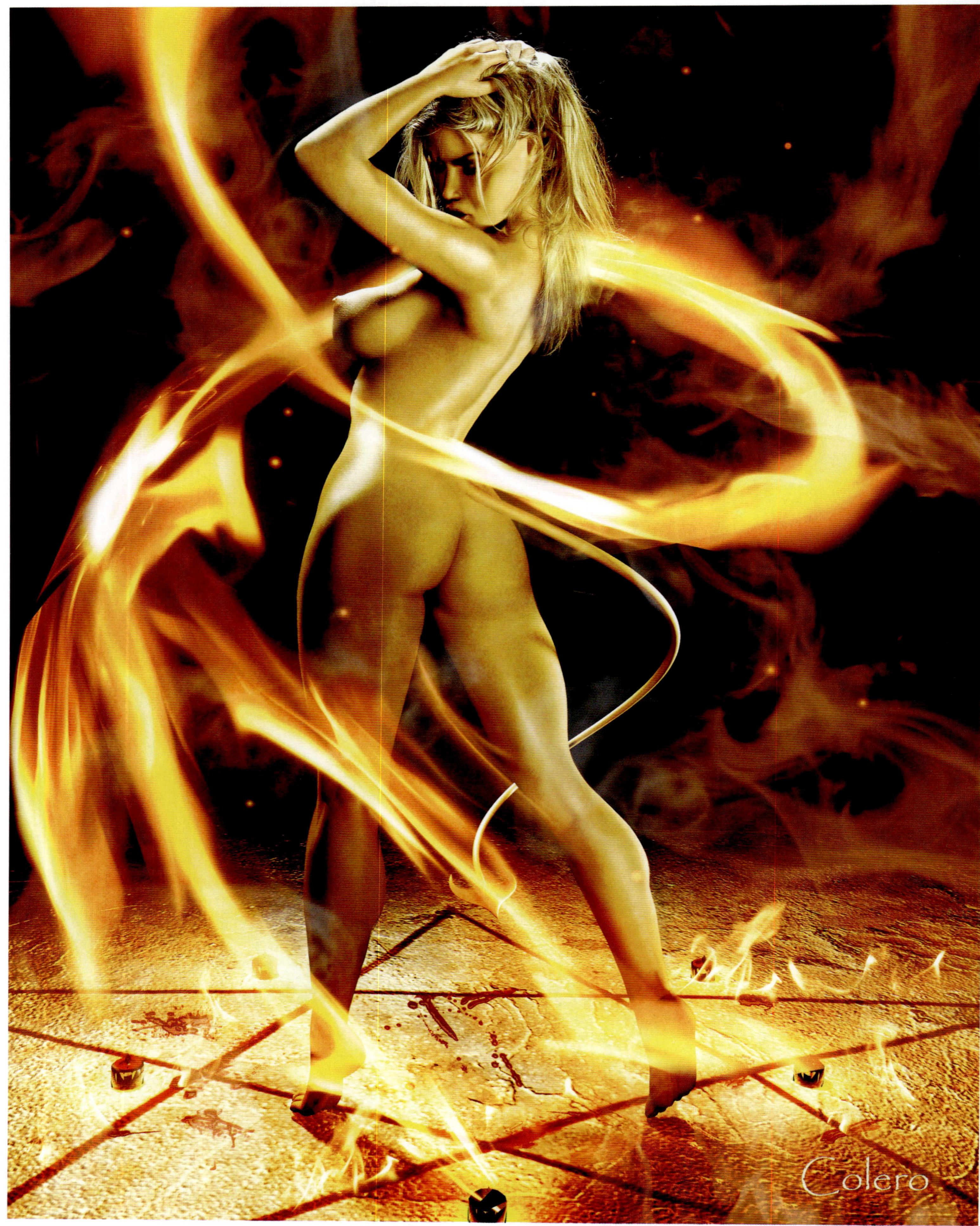

From Hell

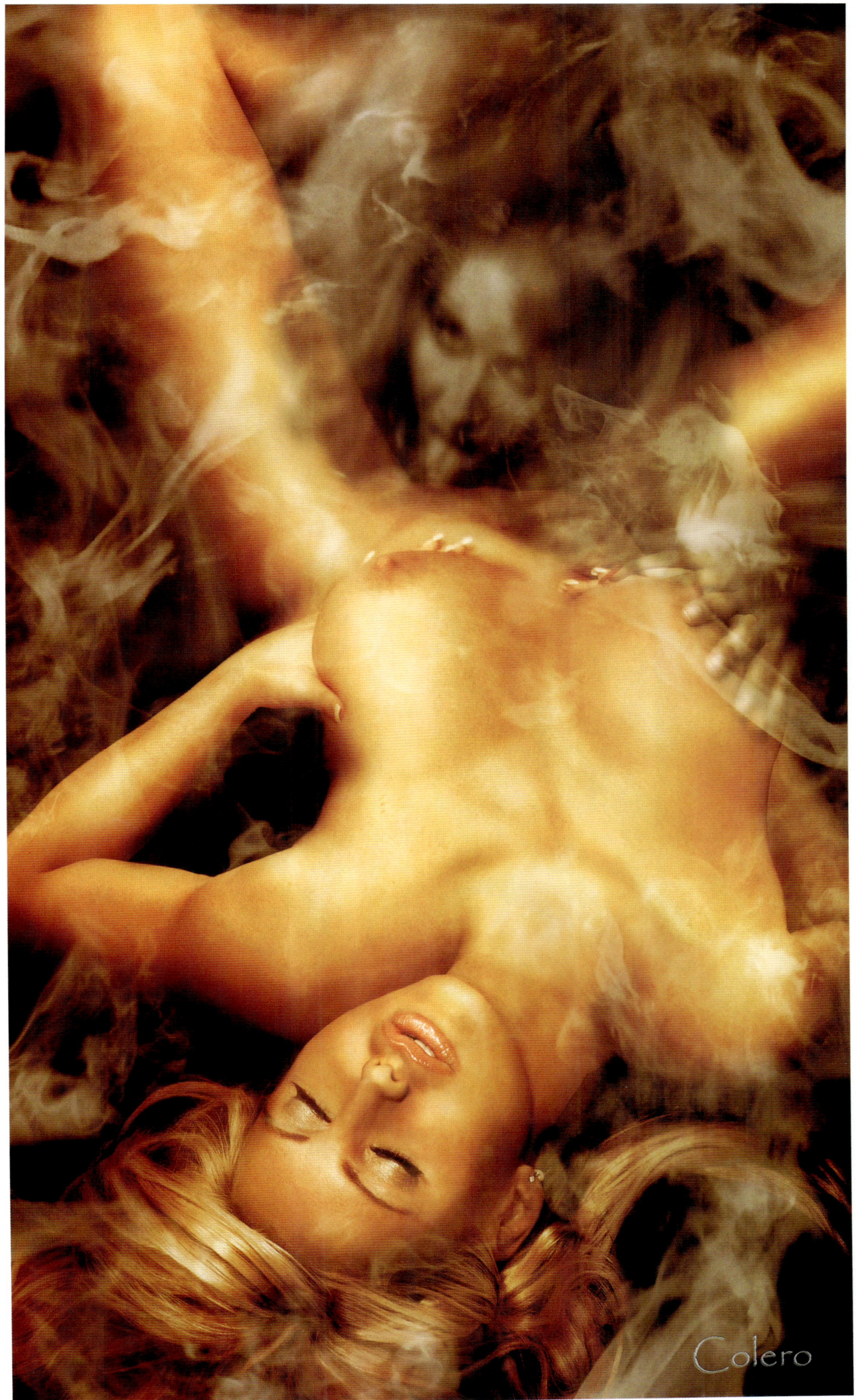

Ghost

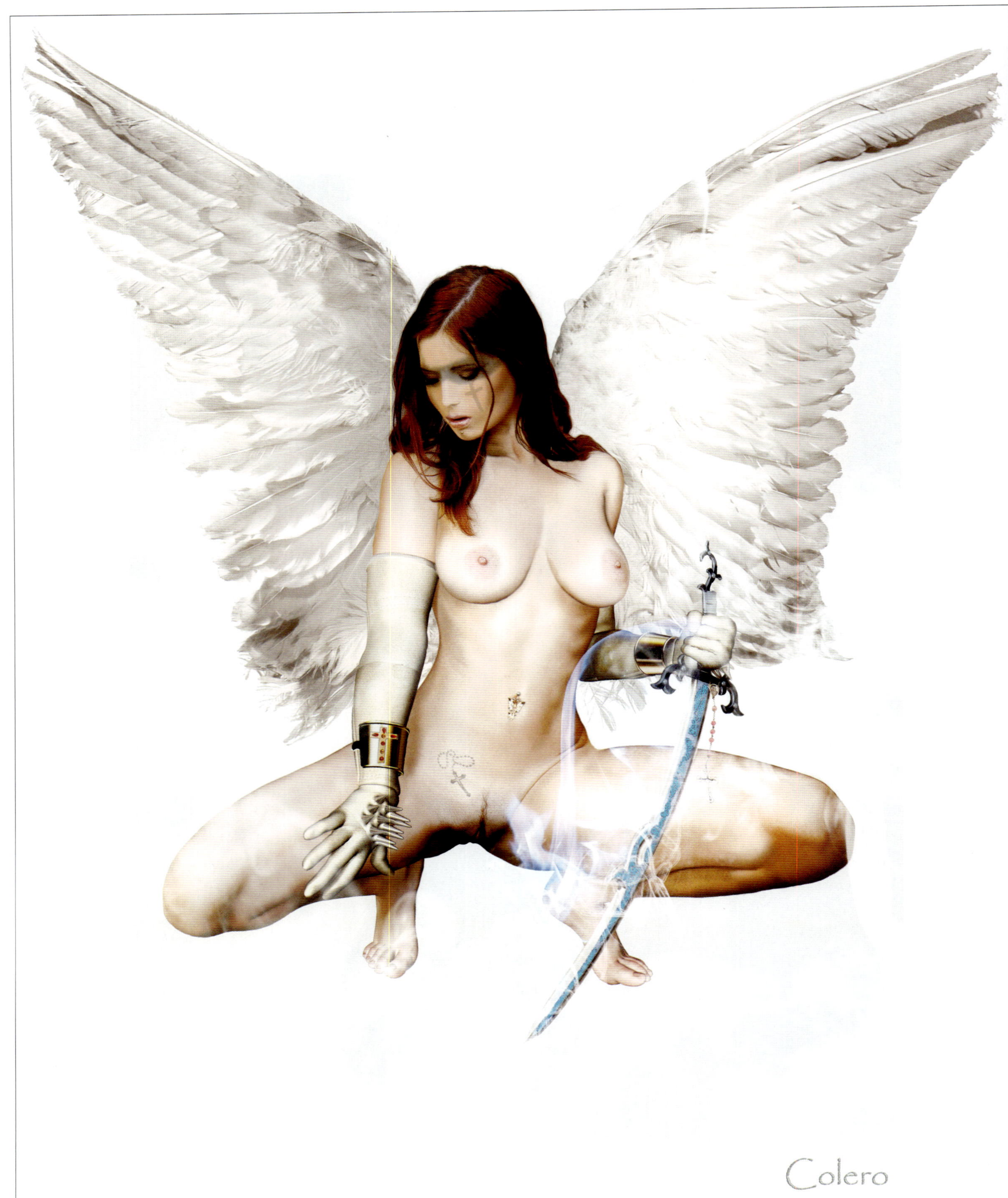

Seraphim

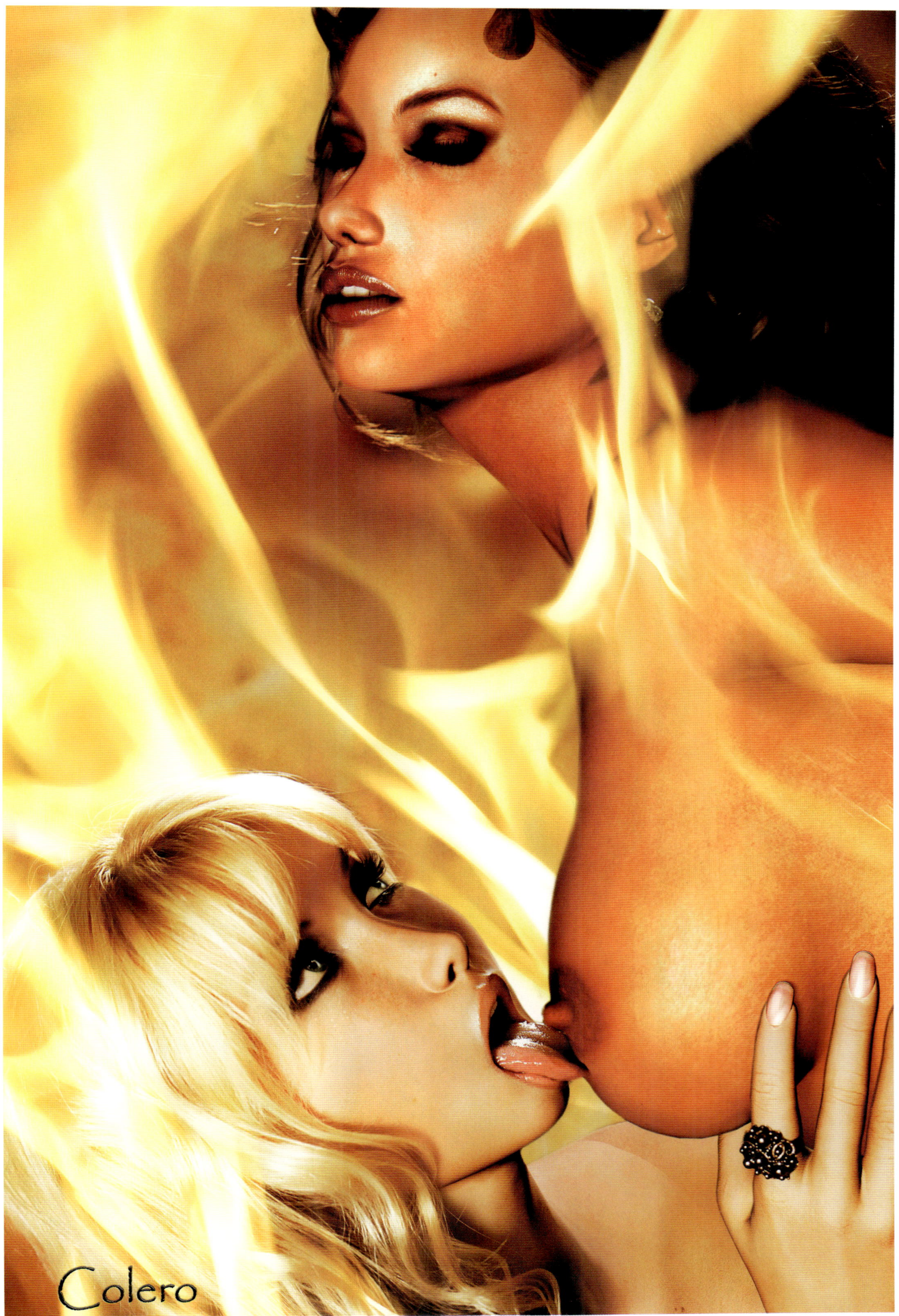

Penance

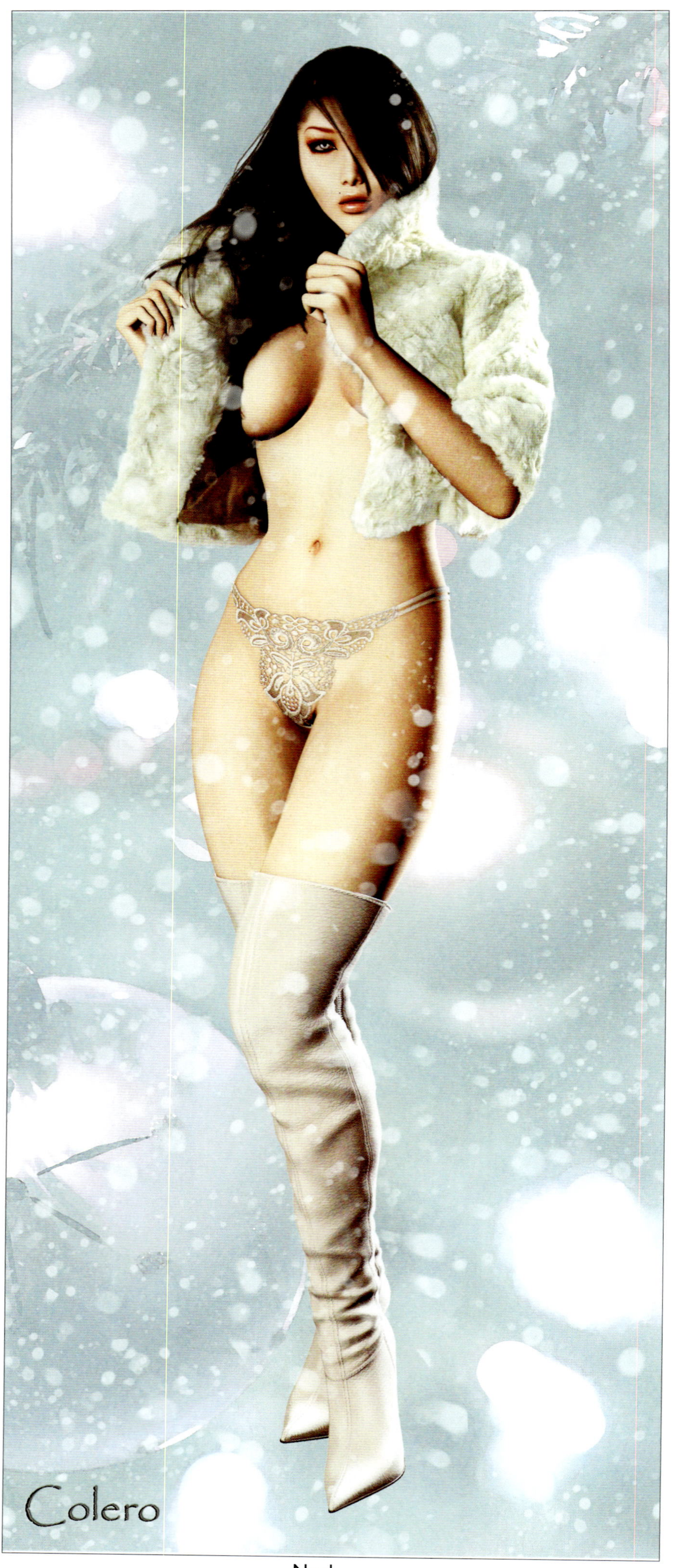

Noel

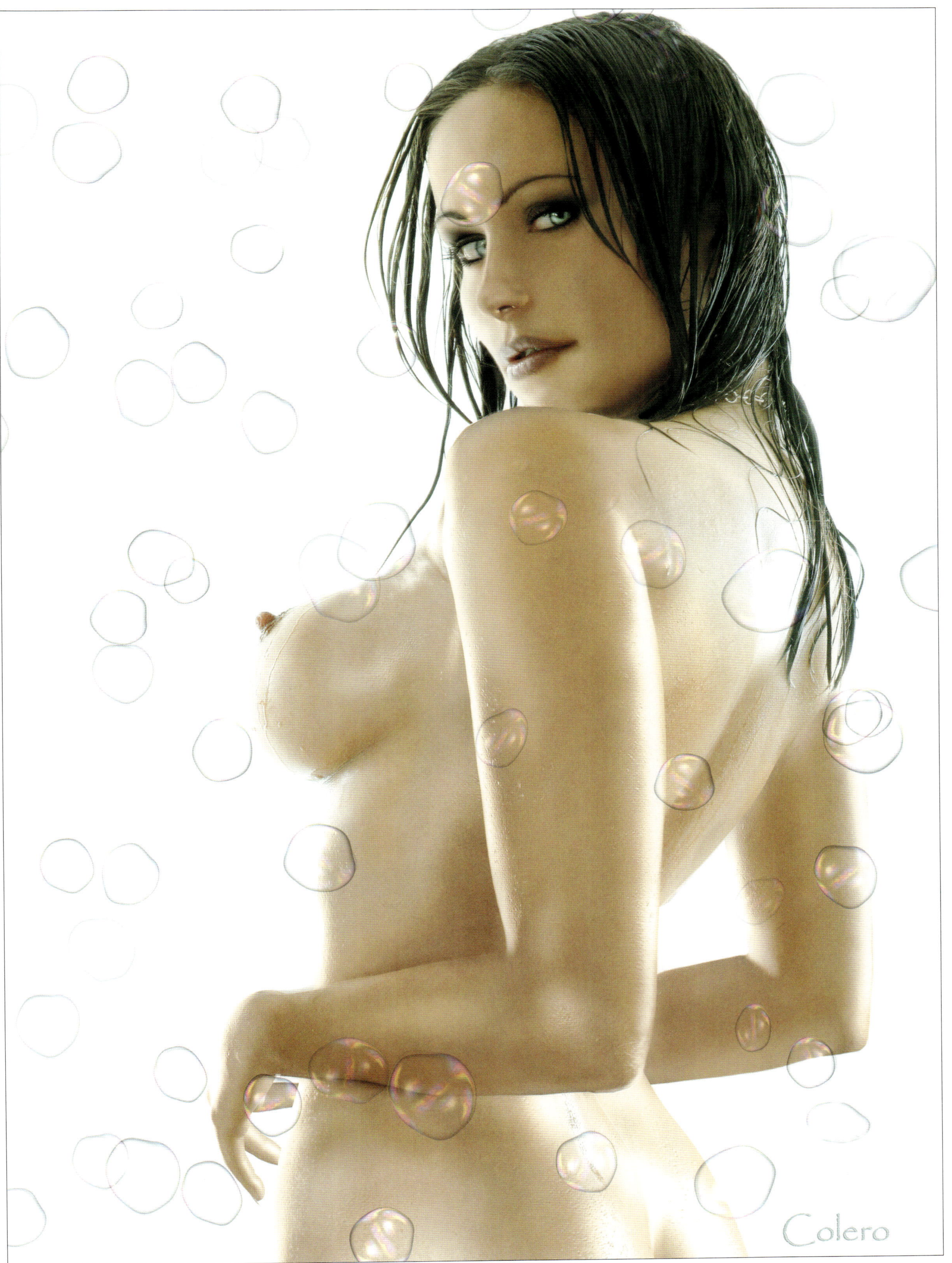

Bubblin'

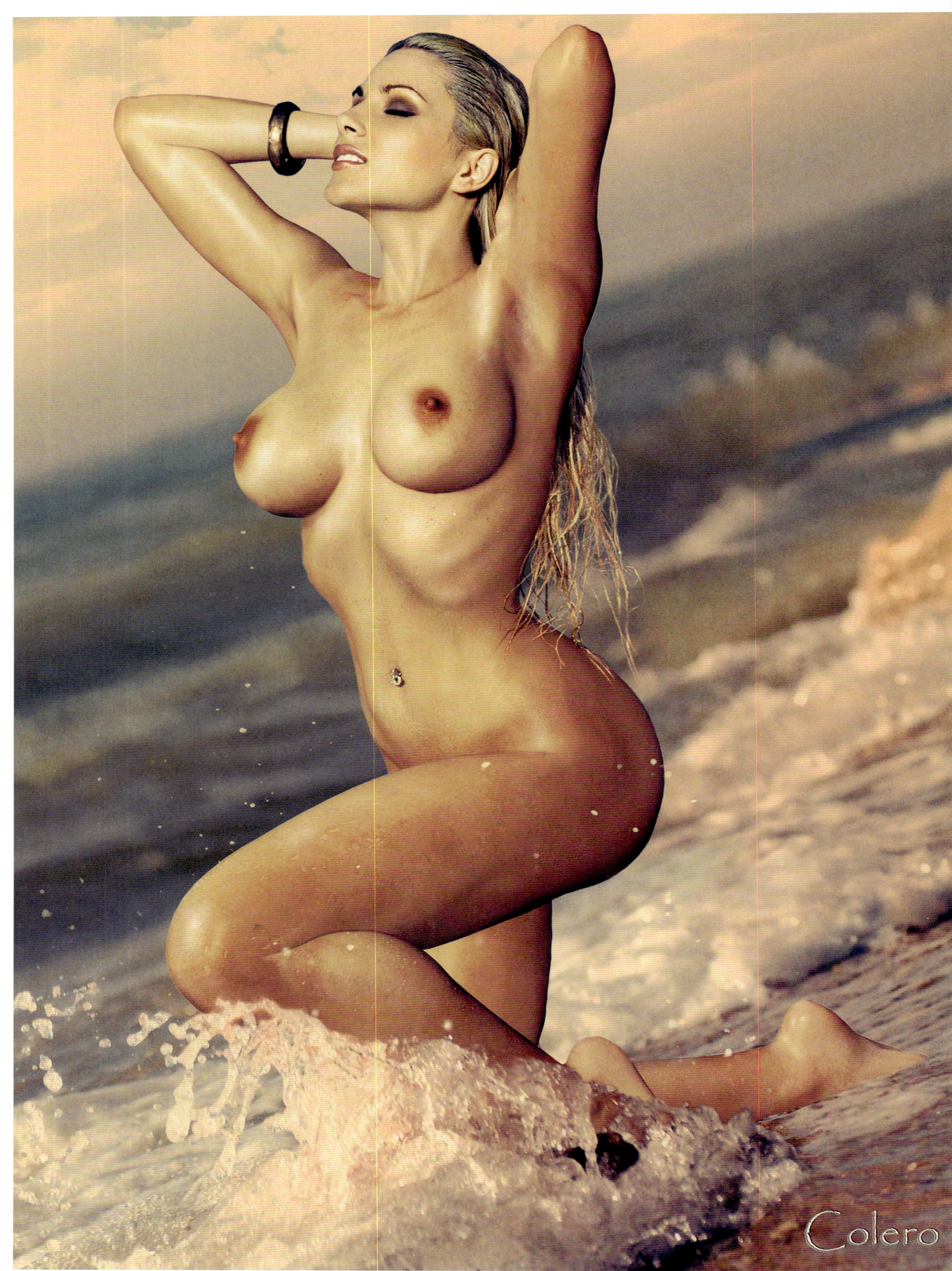

At First Light

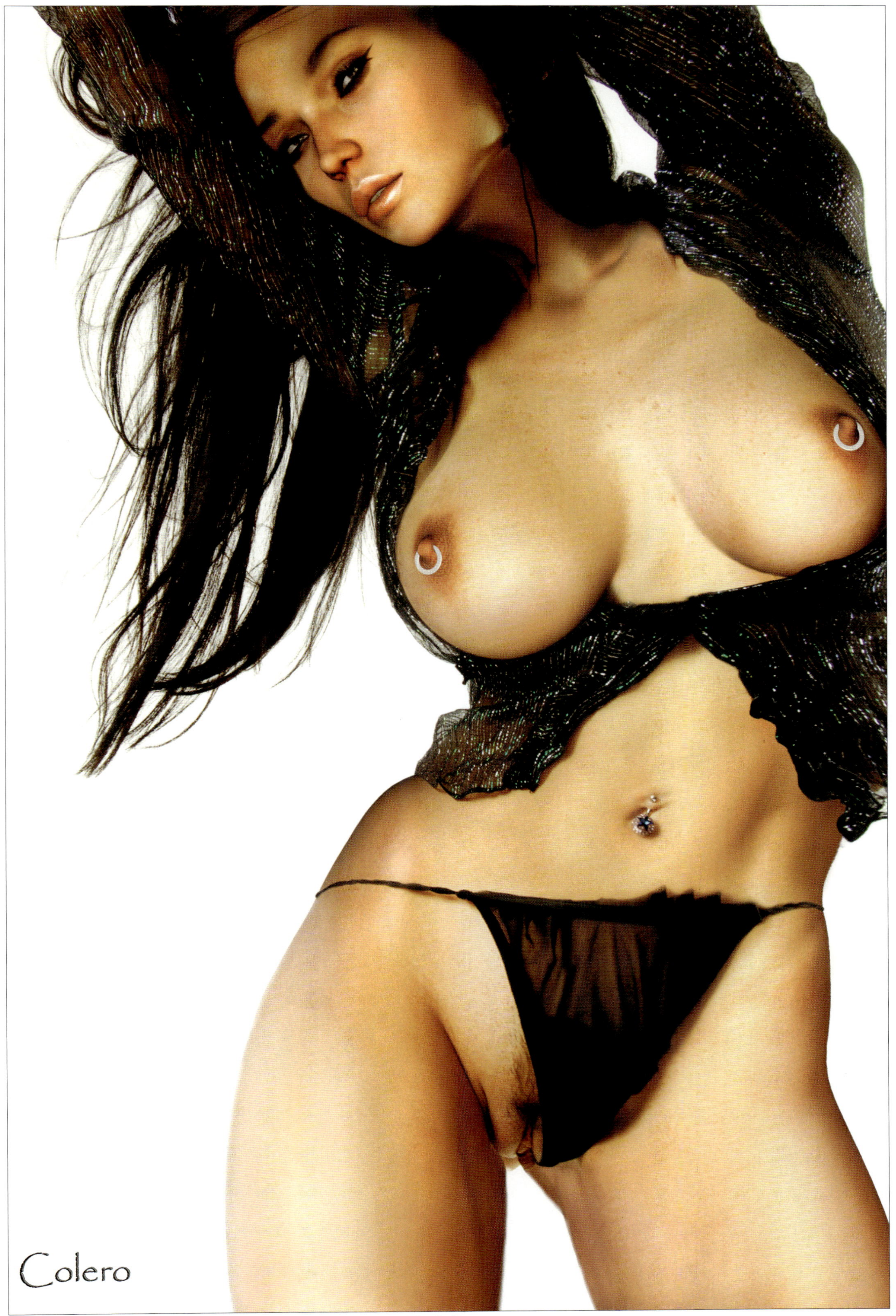

ChickaBoom

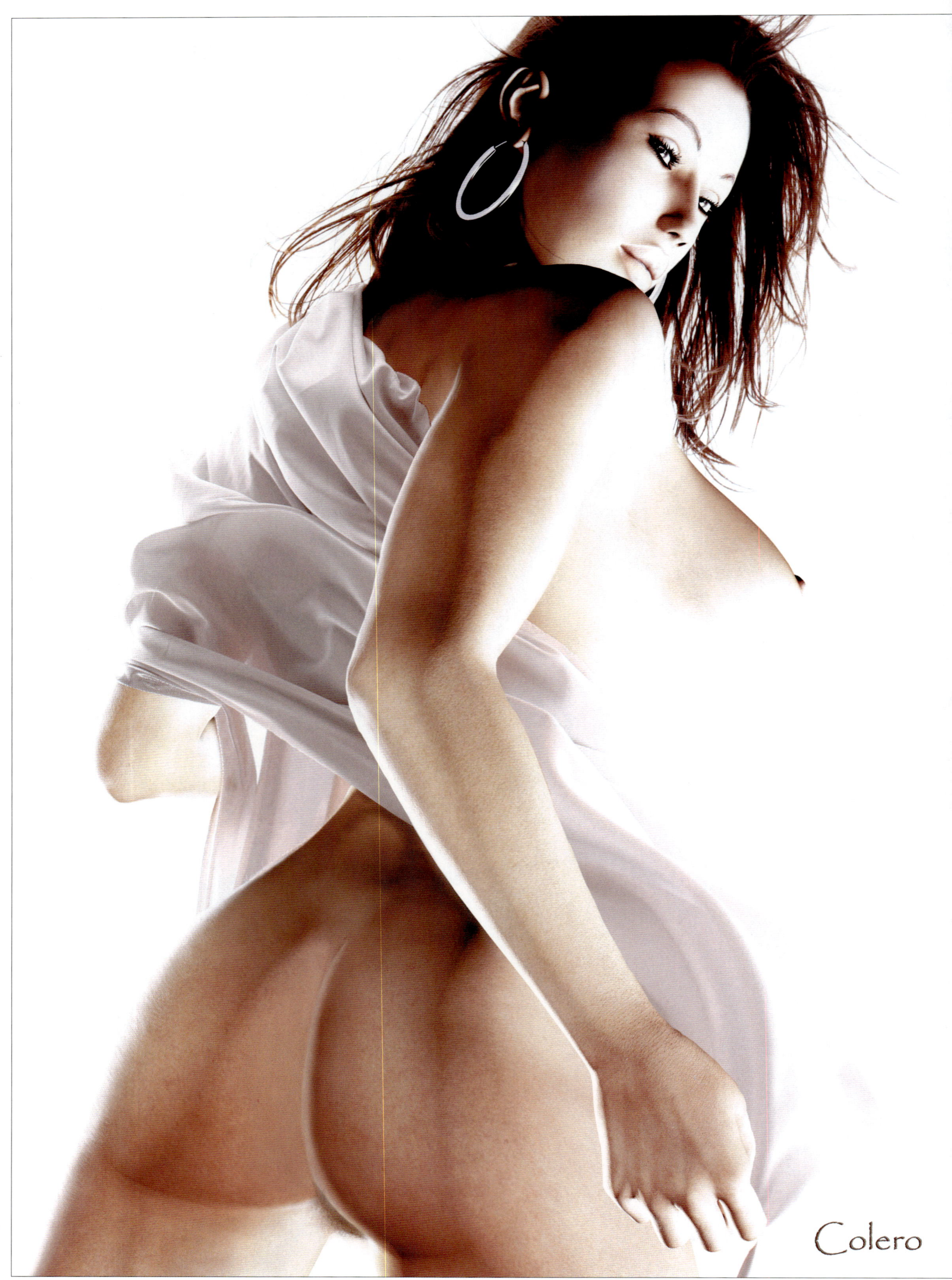

Wrap Her Up